A Short History of Finland

JONATHAN CLEMENTS is the author of a biography of Finland's most famous leader, *Mannerheim: President, Soldier, Spy* (Haus, 2009), as well as *A Brief History of the Vikings* (Robinson, 2005) and *An Armchair Traveller's History of the Silk Road* (Haus, 2013). After living in Finland for over a decade, he became a Finnish citizen in 2021.

A Short History of Finland

by
Jonathan Clements

Sections of this book were first published under the title
An Armchair Traveller's History of Finland in 2014

This revised and updated paperback edition first published in 2022 by
Haus Publishing Ltd, 4 Cinnamon Row, London SW11 3TW

A CIP catalogue record of this book is available from the British
Library

ISBN: 978-1-913368-65-4
eISBN: 978-1-913368-66-1

Typeset in Garamond by MacGuru Ltd

Printed in the United Kingdom by Clays Ltd (Elcograf S.p.A.)

For Tara

Contents

Acknowledgements

Thanks to all those many Finns who have spoken to me about their country over the years, including those many anonymous guides and curators who were unable to resist recounting a few local stories for the mysterious visitor. Thanks also to my two Finnish beta-readers and fact-checkers, Tino Warinowski and Johanna Ahonen, who have done their best to stop me from libelling anyone. Other people who have contributed in some way to this book include Talvikki Aalto, Andrew Deacon, Harry Hall, Aino Haponen, Sanna Heikkinen, Nico Holmberg, Minna Janhonen, Risto Karinkanta, Kirsi Kainulainen, Pekka Kejo, Vantte & Elina Kilappa, Pekka Komu, Jussi Komulainen, Noora Lahtinen, Aleksi Laine, Teemu & Anna-Leena Korpijärvi, Lasse Lilja & Kaisa Aherto-Lilja, Elina Mattila, Samy Merchi, Jani Moliis, Kari Mäki-Kuutti, Kirsi Mäki-Kuutti, Matias Mäki-Kuutti, Pekka Mäki-Kuutti, Raija Mäki-Kuutti, Timo & Seija Mäki-Kuutti, Vitas & Jenni Mäki-Kuutti, Hanna Männikkölahti, Eija Niskanen, Raino & Elina Ojala, Anniina Ouramaa, Ritva 'Oolannin Sota' Parkkonen, Michael Perukangas, Juuso Pesälä, Anna Pitkänen, Marita Pynnönen, Salla Pösö, Ive Riihimäki, Timo Riitamaa, Tuomas Saloniemi, Mari & Mikko Saario, Ellie Shillito, Leena Tarjamo, Anu Uhtio, Niklas Vainio, Harri Virtanen, Myry Voipio, Olli Välke, and Marita von Weissenberg.

In the most convoluted tale of emigration and return, there is the matter of one Heikki Piiparinen, who fled Joensuu in 1917 for a better life in the United States, and never returned home. Instead, he worked at a copper mine, staying at the Finn-run Nikula dormitory in Hancock, Michigan, eventually marrying one of the Nikula girls. Seventy years later, the couple's great granddaughter, Emily Carlson, born into an English-speaking family on the outskirts of Detroit, would discover that she could get cheap tuition in Finland while Googling her ancestral home, return there for her postgraduate degrees, and ultimately became a Finn, shortly before marrying me. Our daughter, Tara, born a Finnish citizen in the last month of 2022, is the latest inheritor of her nation's varied and vibrant history.

Atlantic Ocean

NORWAY

SWEDEN

FINLAND

Gulf of Bothnia

Inari

Rovaniemi

Oulu
(Uleåborg)

Kajaani
(Kajana)

Kuhmo

Kollola
(Karlohy)

Pietarsaari
(Jakobstad)

Iisalmi

Sonkajärvi

Vaasa
(Vasa)

Kuopio

Alavus

Joensuu

Jyväskylä

Savonlinna
(Nyslott)

Tampere
(Tammerfors)

Mikkeli
(Sankt Michel)

Punkaharju

Pori
(Björneborg)

Hämeenlinna
(Tavastelhus)

Lahti

Imatra

Prioz
(Käkisalmi)

Ahvenanmaa
(Åland)

Askainen
(Villnäs)

Turku
(Åbo)

Naantali
(Nådendal)

Vantaa
(Vanda)

Nurmijärvi

Lappeenranta
(Villmanstrand)

Vyborg
(Viipuri)

Porvoo
(Borgå)

Espoo
(Esbo)

Helsinki
(Helsingfors)

Zelenogorsk
(Terijoki)

St P
(Le

Hanko Peninsula

P
(P

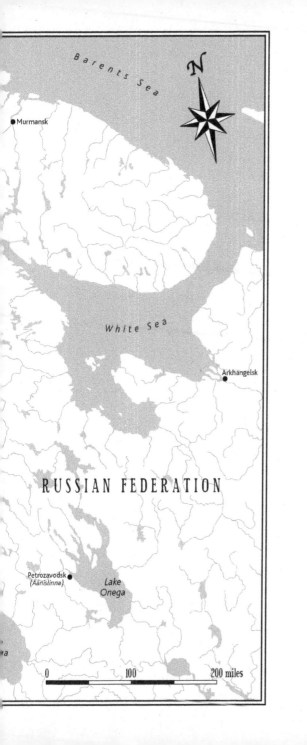

Introduction

The painting hangs in the Kansallismuseo, the National Museum in Helsinki. It depicts a flaxen-haired girl in a white dress and blue scarf on a desolate, storm-tossed shore, clutching a massive book of laws. She is hanging on to it for dear life, while a double-headed eagle attempts to snatch it from her. The eagle's attack is already ripping the pages and warping the cover; it's not clear whether the book or its owner will survive this assault.

The painting is *Hyökkäys* ('The Attack'), completed in 1899 by the thirty-four-year-old artist Edvard 'Eetu' Isto. The story goes that he began work on it in Berlin, but deliberately made the finishing touches in his Finnish homeland, the plight of which he was very pointedly symbolising.

The girl in blue and white is the Maid of Finland, a nationalist icon born in part from the shape made by the country of Finland itself, thought by some to resemble a girl in a dress with her arms outstretched. Her clothes invoke the blue cross of the country's thousands of lakes, on the white snowfield of the Finnish flag. The double-headed eagle represents Imperial Russia, the Tsar of which had also held the position of the Grand Prince of Finland. And the book of laws it is attacking represents almost a century of cordial rulership, in which Finns within the Russian Empire were allowed to use their own language, their own currency, and a limited form of autonomous self-government. Things were changing, and would never quite be the same again.

Hyökkäys was a stark piece of propaganda, part of a massive upswelling of Finnish nationalism that gripped the country in the late nineteenth century. It would end, eventually, in the revolution of 1917, in which Finland became the only former territory of the Russian Empire to evade Soviet takeover.

For the historically minded reader in search of insight into Finland and the Finns, *Hyökkäys* and the National Romantic sensibility that birthed it are part of a pivotal moment. Its artists and authors wrestled with the very nature of 'Finnishness', a concept that had often been ignored or glossed over by two sets of foreign masters. This book similarly follows the Finns' own developing sense of themselves, from hunters and crofters regarded as little more than savages by conquering Swedes, to the initially loyal and welcoming subjects of the Tsar after the Grand Duchy was handed over to Russia. It continues through the turbulent twentieth century, in which Finland was born from the fires of revolution and a bitter civil war, only to be forced to fight for its life in the Winter War, the Continuation War, and the Lapland War.

Because Finland is such a young country, many of its heroes and icons are relatively recent creations. A traveller among the Finns will often spy elements of Swedish or Russian culture, which no Finn will ever believe could not be ineffably Finnish, but also traditions that are less remembered than they are invented or recreated. Paramount among them is the Finnish national myth, the *Kalevala*, one of the first and most influential of many European epics to appear in the nationalist nineteenth century.

With a notoriously difficult language, a legendarily stubborn population, a political scene that aspires to socialist utopia, and international fame for sitting naked in hot, steamy sheds, the people of Finland have an odd reputation. But with the aid of this book, you will see much more of Finland and the Finns – you will hear their own jokes about themselves, and read the words of their songs, and understand the way they view the world.

It has been two decades since I first accidentally went to Finland and inadvertently stayed, eventually becoming a Finn myself. When I was asked to write a history of the country, I set about writing a book that covered the subjects I wish I had known about before I arrived. This book was the result, first published in hardback in 2014 as *An Armchair Traveller's History of Finland*.

For this paperback edition, I have taken the opportunity to expand several sections with new stories, particularly about the fortunes of two very different groups of Finns abroad, those who went to North America, and those who went to (or found themselves in) Soviet Russia. Their story has its links and resonances back home in their fatherland, not least in the way it forms an invisible lobby in those other countries, influencing the attitudes of two large foreign powers towards a small and supposedly insignificant nation.

The Second World War remains such a huge part of Finland's national identity that I had no qualms about expanding my previous chapter with more details of its traditions and historical heritage, while I have also made a deliberate effort to chronicle the doldrum years of the late twentieth century, where 'nothing happened', despite massive changes in Finnish attitudes, society, and culture that often passed the locals by.

1

From the Fenni to Lalli: Prehistory to 1159

The road leads to part of Lake Köyliö in south-west Finland, near the village that also bears that name, winding downhill through a forest park, some distance from the island church. The statue itself seems nondescript and anonymous. From a distance, you'd be forgiven for thinking it was a soldier, standing almost to attention, his left hand holding a long spear. The man is larger than life, clad in furs with a bulky hat more likely to be associated today with the Russian Arctic. In his other hand, resting against his thigh, is a tangle of straps and slats – old-fashioned snowshoes.

He holds an axe under his armpit, as if just about to don the shoes, but keeping his weapon close at hand. One wonders how much fun the Finns have with local visitors, asking them who they think the statue represents. Is it a war memorial? Is it some famous Russian trapper? Is it Mannerheim (if in doubt, say it's Mannerheim), that most famous of Finns, his officer's moustache grown out into a bushy beard on some long mission? Is it a famous Arctic explorer, clutching some kind of harpoon, ready to take on an unlucky whale?

It was sculpted by Aimo Tukiainen in 1989, commissioned

by the local bank, Köyliön Säästöpankki, in celebration of its centenary. You will hear things like this a lot in Finland, a country young enough that not only the subjects, but also the initiators of its public artworks are still acknowledged.

The Finns, perhaps more than many other nations, appreciate the value and use of public art. The statues you see are there for a reason, and the reason is often relatively recent – some bank or factory with a desire to identify itself with older traditions. In this case, the bank chose to make a name for itself by commissioning a statue of an illiterate, brawling country bumpkin, an infamously henpecked husband and murderer. The statue is of a man who may never have even existed, called Lalli.

The Martyrdom of Saint Henry

There are many conflicting stories about Lalli. The original, basic version may not have even given him a name, but during the later Middle Ages the tale was augmented, accreting additional data like a rolling snowball. Whichever way it begins, it ends the same way, sometime around AD 1155, with Lalli, a dim-witted Finnish forester, accosting the saintly Bishop Henry of Uppsala on the winter ice of Köyliö lake. There is a misunderstanding – in the most embroidered of versions, Lalli's wife Kerttu has told him that the bishop came to stay, ate their food, drank their drink, and left 'nothing but ashes'. Lalli swings his axe, and murders the defenceless Henry, inadvertently creating Finland's first martyr and its patron saint.

Lalli hacks off Henry's finger to get at his papal ring. He sticks the bishop's mitre on his head. He rifles through

Henry's positions and returns home to the shrewish Kerttu, boasting of his deed. But when he tries to take the holy hat off, part of his scalp comes with it. His remaining hair starts falling out in clumps. He tries to take off the ring, but it strips the flesh from his finger, leaving only bone. Lalli eventually goes mad, and drowns himself in the lake.

Henry's servants come out of hiding. It is implied that he had ordered them to take refuge in the forest, in the knowledge that Lalli had murderous intent. According to Henry's wishes, they gather up his remains and wrap them in white cloth tied with blue string. Laid on a cart, they are pulled along by a stallion, until it gives up. This is then replaced by an ox. Where the ox stops, a church is built in Henry's memory.

In distant Götaland, Sweden, a priest heard the story of Henry's demise, and made some sort of wisecrack about it. He immediately developed an ominous stomach ache. Before long, more obviously miraculous phenomena began to occur. Two children allegedly rose up from the dead in Finland. A group of sailors prayed to Henry and were saved from a storm. In nearby Kyrö, a lame man walked and a blind woman saw.

By the end of the thirteenth century, Henry, Bishop of Uppsala, was known as Saint Henry, the 'Bishop of Finland', although he had never held that post in life. His unassuming stone cross on Kirkkokari Island in Lake Köyliö has become the starting point of Finland's only Catholic pilgrimage, *Henrikin tie* ('Henry's Road'), along which believers annually walk the 140 kilometres from the site of his martyrdom to Nousiainen, the site of his alleged burial.

On this journey, which ends the night before Midsummer's Eve, travellers are entertained with the *Death-Lay of Henry*, which recounts the events of his life, death, and miracles, in a considerably more sensational fashion than his medieval *Vita Henricus*.

> Now the bishop is in joy, Lalli in evil torture.
> The bishop sings with the angels, performs a joyful
>   hymn.
> Lalli is skiing down in hell. His left ski slides along,
> Into the thick smoke of torture. With his staff he
>   strikes about him:
> Demons beset him cruelly. In the swelter of hell
> They assail his pitiful soul.

But there is no statue of Henry at Köyliö. It's his murderer who gets the permanent memorial, at least in part because Henry was a foreigner. He was a bishop from Uppsala in Sweden, but was widely believed to have come from England.

Garbled references refer to his youth in Cabbage-land (*Kaalimaa*), a non-existent location that has puzzled Finns for centuries. However, any medieval historian is sure to recognise it from an insult directed by Olaf the Stout at poor King Canute about the English food he had to eat. Perhaps there was never a real Henry, either. Like so many other martyrs from before the Congregation on the Causes of Saints in 1588, his canonisation was never officially declared, nor was any diligent Vatican investigator put on his case. The Catholic Church has no record of a Henry of Uppsala that fits in with his timeline, and neither does the Bishopric of Uppsala. It is true that there were English missionaries among the Swedes in the 'New Land' to the east of the Gulf of Bothnia, and indeed likely that more Englishmen rose to prominence in the Church during the reign of the English Pope Adrian IV (r. 1154–9). Although 'Saint' Henry was barely even recognised or celebrated outside Finland, Sweden, and a couple of parishes in north Germany, he achieved his popularity because, in the eyes of the Finnish devout, his story was, at least, local. Finns could point at Lake Köyliö, where he was supposedly killed; they could visit Kyrö, where his early miracles manifested. They could claim him as their own after the fact.

Lalli was a different matter. He was a *local*. He was a Finn who stood up, in some misguided way, to the imposition of authority by Swedish masters. As the years passed, particularly whenever Finns debated 'Finnishness', Lalli cropped up frequently as an icon of all that was not-Swedish, not-foreign, not-Catholic. The statue in Köyliö carefully redacts his iconic image as a thug murdering a holy man, presenting him instead with all the accoutrements otherwise implied by the story: the fur clothes of a trapper, the snowshoes of a wintry landscape, and the axe of a forester. At the most basic of levels, Lalli reduces Finnishness to simple wood-land life in a freezing environment, with a little bit of bloody-minded, murderous resistance to authority thrown in. He is the first of the Finns.

> In wonderful savageness lives the nation of the
> Fenni, and in beastly poverty, destitute of arms,
> of horses, and of homes; their food, the common
> herbs; their apparel, skins; their bed, the earth; their
> only hope in their arrows, which for want of iron
> they point with bones. Their common support they
> have from the chase, women as well as men; for with
> these the former wander up and down, and crave
> a portion of the prey. Nor other shelter have they
> even for their babes, against the violence of tempests
> and ravening beasts, than to cover them with the
> branches of trees twisted together ...

So wrote the Roman author Tacitus in his *Germania*
(AD 98), identifying a tribe far to the frozen north. Fifty
years later, in the *Geographia* (AD 150), the Alexandrian
author Claudius Ptolemy similarly alluded to a tribe he
called the Phinnoi, found in two separate locations in
Scandia and Sarmatia. Both seem in agreement that wher-
ever these Finns are to be found, their life seems rather miserable. This is a recurring concept in discussions of Finland,
a land so far removed from the norms of established culture
that its critics have often found it wanting.

'Foreigners are conceited and envious,' complained Daniel
Juslenius in 1700, 'they foolishly believe that there is no civili-
sation beyond the confines of their own country, and particularly not in these regions, which they have never seen. Indeed,
they boast that their cabins are taller than our towers.'

Humans came relatively late to Finland, since the entire region was buried under ice until only 12,000 years ago. In geological terms, the last of the Ice Ages left Finland so recently that the land is still bouncing back up – lifting in relief after the weight of the snows, and rising fast. Many are the places in Finland where a town named as a harbour, or a mansion named for a beachside view, seem oddly far inland. Many are the historical town records in which townsfolk complain their harbour has become unsuitable, particularly in the north of the Gulf of Bothnia. There, in the eighteenth century, Anders Celsius conducted scientific experiments, and discovered that the coastal land was rising at the geological pell-mell pace of thirteen millimetres a year. By the year AD 4000, the north of the Bay of Bothnia will be a freshwater lake, walled off by a new ridge across its middle.

Archaeological evidence of the first inhabitants of Finland has been lost, drowned, or scraped away by several last gasps of the Ice Age that rolled back over the earliest places of habitation. There is only one place in the region that has offered possible evidence of earlier settlement, and that is the controversial Susiluola ('Wolf Cave') near Karijoki, where archaeologists in 1996 found what may have been evidence of Neanderthal inhabitants some 120,000 years ago. This suggests there were inhabitants in the area between the Riss and Würm Ice Ages. However, Susiluola has become a matter of academic dispute, with some refusing to believe that the limited finds of flint chips are man-made at all, and others arguing that the cave would have been underwater at the time the finds were supposedly left there.

Sometime around 7200 BC, someone left a bone ice pick, a fish net, and a ski runner near the site of modern Lahti. Hunters were converging on Finland from both the south and possibly north, from the Norwegian coast. In Suomusjärvi, now part of Salo in south-west Finland, archaeologists found a Stone Age area of settlement, occupied for around 2,000 years after 6500 BC by humans who subsisted on hunting and fishing. Bone evidence and surviving artefacts suggest that their main prey were seals, perhaps not dissimilar to the endangered Saimaa ringed seal, only 400 of which currently survive – the last descendants of marine mammals left landlocked by the fast-rising lake land.

The world of these Stone Age people was very different, scattered not with the birch and firs of modern Finland, but with hazel, elm, and oak. By 4200 BC, these primitive inhabitants were starting to settle, and trading with nearby tribes. The Comb-Ceramic culture, whose distinctive pots are found across a wide swathe of Europe, made inroads into the Finnish area, and these early users of stone tools began importing a better class of stone from the east – evidence survives in eastern Finland not only of tools made from Russian flint, but of entire slabs of green schist brought from Lake Onega, and wooden spoons made from a pine that only grows near the Urals. We have no idea what the Finns traded for such goods, but later accounts, particularly in Viking sagas, suggest that one of the things that Finland was best known for was animal pelts.

Finland entered the Bronze Age around 1500 BC, when the metal is first found, not mined locally, but brought in as another import. By this time, the archaeological evidence suggests, the Finns had turned to limited farming to supplement their hunting culture, although animal husbandry was more important for them.

So much of the material culture of this period was made from substances that readily decompose. Evidence suggests that all of Finland, along with the rest of the Nordic region, was widely but sparsely settled by the end of the Stone Age, but that the isolated tribes of reindeer herders and seal hunters had a culture much as Tacitus would later describe – of skin tents and wooden utensils, little of which has survived. At some point during the Bronze Age, there was a palpable split between the cultures. Some continued to follow the reindeer herds in the north, living a nomadic existence. Others cleared forest areas and focused on farming. Although the two groups remained closely inter-related, with regular contact and many shared beliefs, their languages began to diverge. We can still hear two accents on what is essentially the same word, used by each of the groups to identify themselves. The herders called their land Sápmi; the farmers called theirs Suomi.

Tacitus thought that the people of Sápmi had the better idea:

> Such a condition they judge more happy than the
> painful idea of cultivating the ground, than the
> labour of rearing houses, than the agitations of hope
> and fear attending the defence of their own property
> or the seizing of that of others. Secure against the
> designs of men, secure against the malice of the
> gods, they have accomplished a thing of infinite

difficulty; that to them, nothing remains even to be wished.

The Rome of Tacitus was far removed from the Finns, although fragments of it did make their way to the far north. A handful of Roman coins have been dug up on Finnish sites, as well as two wine ladles, a glass drinking horn, and a gold bracelet. These items, as well as several swords of Mediterranean origin, appear to have drifted up to Finland through the tribes of Germany, rather than being traded directly with any foolhardy or enterprising Roman merchants.

The Vikings & Balagard

By the Dark Ages, the people of the Suomi farmlands had advanced further to the north, pushing the 'Saami' people of Sápmi out of what is now Tampere and Hämeenlinna. It is possible, although difficult to prove, that this period is the source of certain references in Finnish folklore to Pohjola (the 'Northland'), a rival realm ruled by a wise but vindictive witch-queen, ever at odds with the homespun heroes of Finnish epics.

Slash-and-burn cultivation was the rule – with forest areas cleared, crops sown for several seasons, and the land then abandoned to grow over once more with trees. The Finnish settlers had to contend with visitations from the north and west, as sailors from what is now Norway and Sweden ventured into the lakes. It was in Finland that Norse seamen are liable to have learned one of their most crucial and transferable skills. The skerries and islets of the archipelago in southwest Finland gave way to landlocked lakes and rivers, but portage, in which a ship's crew clambers out and bodily hefts their vessel over a ridge or rapids, opened much of Finland's hinterland to explorers, traders and raiders. By the time we first hear of the semi-legendary foundation of a 'Viking' state in what is now Russia, around the middle of the ninth century AD, it is likely that the rowers who ventured there sailed along a Gulf of Finland that was already either well-settled with homesteads, or entirely picked over for plunder.

Archaeological evidence, once more, is scant, but this itself offers clues as to likely populations. The Åland Islands, close to Sweden, show dense settlement, clear connections to Scandinavia, and grave goods with a substantial amount of silver coins from the Islamic world, suggesting the inhabitants were deeply invested in the slave trade with the caliphate. There is some evidence of settlement, too, in the south-west of Finland, and up through the most easily traversable lakelands, but evidence in the east of Finland is far sparser, usually confined to single uncontextualised finds. Viking swords have been found as far to the east as Kiviniemi, while in 1686, diggers in Uskela (now part of Salo) uncovered a hoard of coins from the Arab world and the England of Ethelred the Unready. Inexplicably tucked away in a corner of the Museum of Central Finland, in Jyväskylä, amid all the anonymous canoes and milk churns, is a striking Viking-era necklace, worn by some long-forgotten lady of a culturally Scandinavian settlement. Traders or returnees from the world beyond certainly left their mark in some of the grave goods, with occasional findings by modern-day archaeologists of glass beads from the Mediterranean, carnelian beads from western Asia, and even a few cowrie shells from the coast of the Indian Ocean. There are even some linguistic shadows – loanwords that can only have arrived in Finland during the era of the Vikings, because they evolved differently later on in Nordic languages – such as the word for a bailer on a ship, *äyskäri* (from the Norse *auskari*).

Viking sagas might allude to 'kings' and chieftains in the lands of lakes and snow, although the word in Finnish for a king (*kuningas*) is a foreign borrowing, as if the Finns themselves never had much of a use for it. But there are occasional leaders of the Finns whose names are mentioned in old legends. Daniel Juslenius, one of Finland's first chroniclers of its own legends, writes of the Finnish 'king' Rostioff, 'who was worshipped as a god by the Swedes after his death', and the feisty princess Skjalv. Dragged back to Sweden as a concubine of King Agne, who had killed her father King Froste, Skjalv bided her time and eventually strangled Ingemar with a golden chain. The *Heimskringla*, chronicle of the Norwegian kings, goes into greater detail:

> Now when King Agne had got drunk, Skjalv bade
> him take care of his gold torc which he had about
> his neck; therefore he took hold of the ornament,
> and bound it fast about his neck before he went to
> sleep. The landtent stood at the wood side, and a
> high tree over the tent protected it against the heat
> of the sun. Now when King Agne was asleep, Skjalv
> took a noose, and fastened it under the ornament.

Thereupon her men threw down the tent-poles, cast
the loop of the noose up in the branches of the tree,
and hauled upon it, so that the king was hanged
close under the branches and died; and Skjalv with
her men ran down to their ships, and rowed away.

Daniel Juslenius, in his version of the tale, adds the words,
'*postea revertens domum praeda onusta*' ('and then returned
home laden with booty'), suggesting that the original events
that informed the tale might have involved more elements
of a raid than a quest for revenge.

Far more common in saga sources are references to
sorcerers and witches with some Finnish connection,
but their provenance is doubtful, as is their location. The
Norse skalds used the term 'Finn' to refer to both Saami
and Suomi peoples, so many of the tales from the sagas take
place in a vague area somewhere between northern Norway
and Russia.

Norse sailors made it as far as the Tammer rapids, the
site of modern Tampere, where one more heave of a ship up
the steep slope would open up the multiple routes through
northern lakes. The site of Tampere's modern airport, Pirkkala, still bears a name that may derive from Birca, the
Birch Island trading post of old Sweden, evoking images of
ships pulled ashore, campfires, and haggling over furs. This
Norse presence is marked, in a typically Finnish fashion,
with a statue not of the visitors, but of the type of local who
greeted them – the *Hunter*, one of four statues by Wäinö
Aaltonen on Tampere's modern Hämeensilta bridge, in
which a bronze, naked man holds out an animal skin. To

this day, the word in Finnish for money is *raha* (literally 'pelt'), and *oravannahka* ('squirrel skin') is a jocular slang term for cash.

The Norse visitors adapted their sea-borne methods for river travel, seizing islands mid-stream or mid-lake as naturally defended bases. Somewhere in what is now Finland, there was an island fort, called Balagard (possibly 'Meadow Fort') by the Dark Age Scandinavians, but its location is unclear. Ice and changing water levels have probably long done for any material evidence of it, leaving much discussion of Finland in Viking sagas a matter of vague generalities. The land of the Finns crops up in occasional stories, where trips in search of 'tribute' from the forest region led to the extraction of furs and pelts from the huntsmen. Finland also seemed to be a place of piracy and adventure, where several Danish and Norwegian rulers sailed in search of their fortunes, usually at the expense of the local residents.

The youngest child of Siward, King of the Geats, the princess Alvild, for example, was said to walk everywhere veiled by her cloak, in order to hide her fabled beauty from unwelcome suitors. Her father did his bit to protect his daughter's chastity by posting armed guards outside her chambers and, just to be sure, giving her two poisonous snakes to keep as pets – these deadly creatures forming the last line of defence.

The story, purporting to refer to events in the fifth century AD, appears in Saxo Grammaticus's *History of the Danes* as well as Olaus Magnus's *Description of the Northern Peoples* – the latter largely rips off the former. Both versions seem a little garbled, with Alvild's guardians soon repurposed not as a protection from suitors, but as a test that suitors must overcome. True to the tradition of difficult father-in-laws in many cultures, Siward promises his daughter's hand to anyone who can run the gauntlet, although any who give up halfway will be beheaded and have their heads stuck on a spike.

The Danish prince Alf somehow makes it through and slays the snakes with a red-hot spear-point, to Alvild's delight. Alvild's mother upbraids her for being so shallow as to like a man merely for his looks (and snake-slaying capabilities), and persuades her to renounce all suitors, disguise herself in men's clothes, and run away to become a pirate. She manages this by handily stumbling across a group of Vikings who have just lost their leader, and who inexplicably decide that a freshly arrived princess would make an ideal replacement. She then marauds all along the coast of Finland, until one fateful day on its south-western tip, off the Hanko peninsula (the only time an actual Finnish place-name crops up), she spies a rival fleet heading towards the port. Alvild orders her fleet onto the attack, in a fierce battle of locked oars and onboard swordplay.

Despite, it is implied, numerous victories in her Viking career, Alvild finally meets her match, when the rival Viking leader storms aboard her ship accompanied by overwhelming numbers of fresh warriors. But when his lieutenant Borkar knocks off Alvild's helmet, Alf, for it is he, realises the true identity of his foe.

> [Alf], as soon as he saw the delicacy of her
> countenance, realised that they should be going to

work with kisses, not with weapons; they should
lay aside their hard spears and handle their foe with
more persuasive attentions.

In something of an anti-climax, at least for me, Alf immediately sticks Alvild back in a dress and drags her home to live
happily ever after – their daughter, Gurith, becoming one
of the ancestors of the kings of Denmark.

The eleventh-century chronicler Adam of Bremen, like
many fellow authors who touched on Finnish subjects, was
keener on pointing out that the people of Lapland were
pagan sorcerers:

These people, it is said, are to this day so superior in
the magic arts or incantations that they profess to
know what everyone is doing the world over. Then
they also draw great sea monsters to shore with a
powerful mumbling of words and do much else of
which one reads in the Scriptures about magicians.
All this is easy for them through practice. I have
heard that women grow beards in the extremely
rough alps of that region, and that the men live in
the woods, rarely exposing themselves to sight.

Adam is on his own in his account of bearded ladies (and
indeed 'alps', since Finland has no actual mountains), but
he was the inheritor of a long tradition of tall tales about
Finnish wizardry, much of which can be found in the
Viking sagas. There are garbled tales, preserved among the
ancient manuscripts of Iceland, of 'Finns' who could leave

their bodies in a drug-induced trance, flying in the form of birds of prey, or making long voyages in the form of whales.

Finnvitka, the 'making of witchcraft', seems to have been the preserve of the people of Lapland, such that in modern Swedish, the phrase 'pay a visit to the Finns' survives as a term for visiting a fortune teller. In *Heimskringla*, the chronicle of the kings of Norway, it's a Lappish witch who foretells the colonisation of Iceland, and a group of shape-shifting Saami shamans who reconnoitre the island as whales before the trip is approved.

Perhaps the most famous graduate of the Finnish wizardry school was Gunnhild Kingsmother, a tenth-century woman of royal Scandinavian birth, who was packed off to Lapland to learn magic from Saami shamans. Depending on which saga one believes, she was either staying as a guest with 'Motull, King of the Finns', or living in some sort of sexualised bondage in a shack with two predatory warlocks. Either way, she ran into the ominously named Erik Bloodaxe, who whisked her away back to Norway, where he eventually became king, as would their son Harald Greycloak.

Gunnhild looms large in many of the most famous Icelandic sagas, where she is often depicted as a spiteful termagant. It has been suggested that her Finnish origins, coming from the mysterious and feral lands of the north and east, were concocted by later writers in order to both explain her bad behaviour, and to help shift the blame on to her for political decisions that were actually made by her husband.

The name Balagard crops up in *Heimskringla* in the saga of Olaf the Saint (995–1030), when the future king of Norway, as a teenage hoodlum, takes part in a skirmish at what *may* have been Hirdal, about twenty miles west of modern-day Helsinki. The locals initially give as good as they get, killing a number of Olaf's men in forest combat, until, 'during the night, the Finns with their witchcraft made a furious gale and a storm at sea.'

> Stern was the third storm-of-
> Steel, what time the king in
> Her Dale forest fought the
> Finnish hordes in combat.
> But in the east, the ocean's
> ebb-shore parted the Vikings
> Past Balagard's beaches
> Beat the liege's sea-stags.

That, at least, is the accurate translation by Lee Hollander in his *Heimskringla*. Samuel Laing's somewhat freer version throws away much of the more obscure poetic kenning devices in order to make it rhyme, but also makes what happened a little clearer.

> The third fight was at Herdaler, where
> The men of Finland met in war
> The hero of the royal race,
> With ringing sword-blades face to face.
> Off Balagard's shore the waves
> Ran hollow; but the sea-king saves
> His hard-pressed ship, and gains the lee
> Of the east coast through the wild sea.

There was a movement, among Swedish-speaking Finns in the nineteenth century, to establish that they were the descendants of such Vikings, but this claim was only true in the most roundabout way, in the sense that their own ancestors arrived *from Sweden* in new waves of settlers, after the Viking era proper had ended. Despite rich allusions in the sagas, settlements in parts of Finland during the Viking era were not necessarily enduring. Finland's western and southern coasts and the Åland Islands were certainly part of the Viking world up until the tenth century, but then seem to have suddenly ebbed away. Changes in climate, disease, or even opportunities elsewhere may have lured away many permanent settlers, turning references to Finland once more into occasional asides about a 'wilderness' where hunting parties might make seasonal forays. It has even been suggested that such 'hunting parties' were not only local settlers in search of furs, but actual Vikings in search of slaves, thereby rendering life on the Finnish coast a precarious and ultimately transient existence.

A memorial runestone in Hämlinge, Sweden, for example, raised sometime around 1050, attests:

> Brusi had this stone erected in memory of Egill, his brother. And he died in *Tafæistaland* whence Brusi brought the land's levy in memory of his brother.

The meaning of the inscription is slightly vague – we can see that the luckless Egill died in Tavastia, itself liable to have derived from the old Finnish *taustamaa* (the 'hinterland'), but nobody can tell if Brusi subsequently went there to avenge him, or if the pair of them had been on a trip to avenge a third, unnamed brother. The phrase 'brought the land's levy' is similarly unclear, and can mean anything from extorting money with menaces, to collecting tax, to leading an army.

The Newborn King

There is a marked change to the archaeological record in Finland in the Middle Ages, as a palpable *absence* sweeps from west to east across the country. Sometime around the middle of the eleventh century, the people of the Åland Islands in the Baltic stopped burying their dead with grave goods. Whereas bodies had previously been accompanied by artefacts for use in the afterlife – swords and armour, farming implements, and spinning paraphernalia, even sometimes animal sacrifices – now archaeologists were lucky to find anything in a grave beyond a simple necklace with a crucifix.

Only a few decades later, the same practice arrived in south-west Finland ('Finland Proper', as it is still called), where the former Swedish settlers were supplanted by new arrivals who had given up on paganism. Some pagan grave-yards were abandoned altogether. Others instead gained a grander new centrepiece in the form of a Christian church, defiantly situated on top of all the ancestors, both breaking with the old ways and claiming to inherit them.

Within a hundred years, the new religion had spread up into Tavastia – the old name for the long reach of lands towards Hämeenlinna and Tampere. However, burial practices further to the east, in Karelia, remained pagan until around 1300.

Many centuries later, the folklorist Elias Lönnrot (see Chapter 3) would collate some of the surviving tales, songs, and poems from Karelia that alluded to the arrival of Christianity with confusion. His *Kalevala* collection ends with the song cycle of the 'Newborn King', in which a pious virgin called Marjatta eats a magical berry that makes her pregnant, is cast out by her family, and gives birth to a child prodigy that the sun and moon praise as being their own creator.

She goes off to Väinämöinen, the Finnish hero, to ask him what she should do, and he sternly orders that the baby be thrown in a swamp. The child then speaks, upbraiding Väinämöinen and calling him a stupid old man whose time has passed. After a tongue-lashing that lasts for a couple of pages, Väinämöinen gets into his boat and sails away in a huff. It is meant to be a happy ending, in which the Christ-child brings light to the forests, and the old ways depart leaving only their music, but Väinämöinen's parting words bear about them an element of prophecy and curse – a rather confident prediction that the time will come when the Finns will call him back.

> Suns may rise and set in Suomi,
> Rise and set for generations,
> When the North will learn my teachings,
> Will recall my wisdom-sayings,
> Hungry for the true religion.
> Then will Suomi need my coming,
> Watch for me at dawn of morning,
> That I may bring back the Sampo,

Bring anew the harp of joyance,
Bring again the golden moonlight,
Bring again the silver sunshine,
Peace and plenty to the Northland.

Before political authority arrived from Sweden on the point of a sword, the forests and farms of Finland experienced a slow and unstoppable rise of Christian conversion, washing from west to east.

Elements of Christianity were first intermixed with Finland's original pagan religion, and survive in many folktales and spells that modern-day Finns might sheepishly prefer to call prayers. There are stories that Christ arrived among the trees, and baptised the son of Tapio, Finland's god of the forests. Jesus, or Christ (but never Jesus Christ), and Mary are often invoked in cantrips for healing wounds, staving off gossips, or warding off evil.

Lönnrot's *Magic Songs of the Finns* (1880) recorded all these atavisms, still recounted in the wilds of Karelia in his day, as well as many mixtures of half-understood tales of Christian saints with half-remembered tales of pagan gods.

A spell for luring otters into traps conflates Christopher, 'the golden king of rivers', with a Finnish river god. Tahvanus, an equestrian god, is conflated with Tapani, the Finnish pronunciation of Stephen, in a spell that exhorts Saint Stephen to watch over a group of horses. Juhannes, the 'best of priests', refuses to baptise the children of the witch-queen of Lapland, but christens fire itself, turning the fiery pyres of every Finnish midsummer's eve (*Juhannus*) from a pagan festival into a Christian celebration.

Surviving stories from the fall of paganism also allude to the growing power of the Christian community, and the sense that baptism eventually became not only desirable, but a prospect that could be withheld from the undeserving. One snippet contains a warning from an exorcist to an evil spirit, suggesting that:

> If thou shouldst injure a Christian man or destroy
> a man that is baptised, christening perchance will
> injure thee, baptism will haply thee destroy.

Already, the story was spreading that Lalli had paid dearly for his murderous assault on Bishop Henry. There would surely be other martyrdoms in the expansion of Christianity into the forests, but the priests were soon followed by crusaders and colonists. As the kingdom of Sweden advanced ever eastward, and the proto-Russian state of Novgorod pushed westwards to meet it, the Finns were caught in the middle. They faced contending forms of Christianity and allegiance that would buffet them for the next thousand years.

2

East of Sweden: 1159–1809

In the town square of Vyborg, in what is now Russia, there is a statue of a noble-looking warrior. He stands proud, his sword held nonchalantly, blade down, like a walking stick, his chest raised as if preparing to bellow out a command to the castle on the other side of the nearby strait. His helmet has an odd crest to it, and his face is a sea-dog scramble of beard and moustache.

This is Torkel Knutsson (d. 1306), a Swedish military leader who chose this spot to build a coastal island-fortress like the Viking strongholds of old. Torkel had led what is now usually known as the Third Swedish Crusade, pushing back the peoples of Novgorod and establishing a new border for Sweden many hundreds of miles further to the east than it sits today. The area was hotly contested for many centuries to come, and indeed, was not even acknowledged as Swedish territory until a generation after Torkel's death. The statue was raised in 1908, in what was then the Finnish city of Viipuri, but removed and sequestered in a cupboard in 1944. Now it is back in full view, gazing proudly at the nearby castle.

The Imaginary Crusades

The 'First' Swedish Crusade, in which Saint Henry supposedly met his end, remains a matter of conjecture. Quite possibly it never happened, or is a hopeful spin on far more mundane raids and expeditions into the Finnish marches. The incorporation of Finland, officially and politically, into Swedish territory, did not truly occur until around 1249, when Birger Magnusson (1200–66), 'Duke of the Swedes', led a campaign among the lakes, recorded a century later in a German chronicle as the official date of the pacification of the Finnish lands, when Finland was brought under Swedish authority. It was only then, with Finland secure, that Swedish legends began backdating this acquisition, rebranding Birger's achievements as a 'Second' Crusade in the footsteps of a mythical first.

Sweden appears to have embarked upon this large-scale deception to scare off potential competitors. Since Finland was, as far as the Swedes were concerned, unclaimed wilderness, it might appear to be fair game to representatives from any number of kingdoms. The Swedes were not alone – their expeditions had to contend with similar forays by the kingdom of Denmark, which eventually concentrated on the southern shore of the Gulf of Finland. Meanwhile, the proto-Russian state of Novgorod was expanding westwards into the same territory. Largely forgotten in all the posturing and combat of the period is the contribution of the Germans, whose Hanseatic League of merchants enjoyed powerful trading connections all along the Baltic coasts without seeking any particular political power.

These merchants from Saxony and Westphalia, who

began arriving in southern Finland with artefacts of technology and culture in the thirteenth century, have left very little evidence of their presence, although Finnish slang of the period referred to any item of intricacy or wonder as *saksa* ('German'). It's the Germans who are thought to have built the first church in Turku, and who supplied much of the trade goods that flowed into south-west Finland to make culture there possible in the first place.

Sweden's sudden decision to pretend to have been running around in the forests, Bible in one hand and sword in the other, for the previous hundred years or so, should be taken in the context of these contending cultural influences, as a long-term move designed to keep the Danes and Germans away from the Finnish shores. In this they were successful, so much so that many Finns are not aware that there was any competition at all.

A 'Third' Crusade duly followed, although as ever, the term 'crusade' seems overly hopeful, and was often retroactively applied to random skirmishes and occasional sallies in the centuries-long to-and-fro between the peoples of Sweden and their rivals in Novgorod. So it is that we have the chronicles of the Russians recording a stirring victory against the 'Swedes' in 1240, when Prince Alexander Nevsky gained his surname for utterly destroying the enemy at the Battle of the River Neva. As related in the *First Chronicle of Novgorod*:

> Swedes came with a great army, and Norwegians and
> Finns and Tavastians with ships in great numbers,
> and they stayed on the Neva ... willing to take

[Lake] Ladoga, and to put it short, Novgorod and all of its lands. But still protected the merciful, man-loving God and sheltered us from the foreign people ... Prince Alexander did not hesitate at all, but went against them with Novgorodians and people of Ladoga ... And a great number of them fell; and when [the Swedes] had loaded two ships with the bodies of high-born men, they let them sail to the sea; but the others that were unnumbered, they cast to a pit, that they buried; and many others were wounded; and that same night they fled, without waiting for the Monday night, with shame.

This will be news to anyone reading similar chronicles from Sweden, which make no mention of any crusade, nor any great battle, let alone a great defeat on the Neva. The Swedes at the time were far too busy fighting a war amongst themselves about the rightful heir to the Swedish throne, making it highly unlikely that anyone would be in a position to mount a large expedition against the Russians.

Notably, the chronicle mentions 'Tavastians', people from the hinterland near what is now Hämeenlinna and Tampere. Only three years earlier, in 1237, a papal letter to the archbishop of Uppsala had suggested that the Swedes go on a crusade in Tavastia, to protect Christian settlers from raiders – possibly from Novgorod, but more likely other Finns. This seems to run in the same tradition as an earlier papal admonition, from 1172, which complained about the number of fair-weather Christians in Finland, happy to continue their pagan ways when life was good, but whining to the nearest bishop that they were under threat whenever attacked by raiders. One place-name in modern Finland is a distant echo of such prevarications – Katumajärvi, near modern Hämeenlinna, literally translates as 'Lake of Regret', and is thought to have been the place where locals would wash off the taint of their Christian baptism after their crusader rescuers retreated once more to the south.

On the basis of all this evidence, or lack of it, it seems reasonable to suggest that the Finnish hinterland remained as uncontrolled and subject to changes in authority as it had done during the Viking era. Isolated pockets were claimed by Novgorod, although such an advance led to claims in Sweden that Novgorodians had 'attacked' Swedish territory. The next season, Swedes would take back 'their' town or trading post, only for the Novgorodians to report the act as an attack by raiders. Any Finnish settlers caught in the middle would be buffeted by seasonal changes in allegiance, told first that they were Eastern Orthodox Russians, and then that they were Catholic Swedes. A picky historian might also note that when Alexander Nevsky led an army that included 'people of Ladoga' against an army that included 'Tavastians', he was essentially leading one group of ethnic Finns against another.

The Danish King Valdemar II (1170–1241), instigator of the Livonian crusade, either travelled himself, or sent high-ranking minions on a tax-collecting mission across the Baltic, starting in Denmark but taking in the newly conquered lands around faraway Tallinn, in what is now Estonia. The route was outlined in a Latin document, sometimes termed the *Liber census Daniae* (*The Danish*

Census Book), or *King Valdemar's Itinerary*, which describes the route to Tallinn in a series of coastal hops, taking in the Åland Islands and southern Finland.

> *De arnholm transmare aland usque lynæbøte.*
> *Inde usque thiyckækarl. Notandum est quod inter*
> *thiyckækarl et lynæbøte multe iacent insule fyghelde*
> *nomine. Inde usque aspæsund et ibi sunt tres insule*
> *quarum una est aspæ, secunda refholm, III:a malmø*
> *et iurima iacet ultima ab eis uersus australem plagam*
> *et proxima mari.*

From Arholma over the sea to Åland and thence to Lynæbøte [modern Lemböte]. From there to Thiyckækarl [Kökar]. It can be noted that between [these places] there are many islands called Fyghelde [Föglö]. From there to Aspæsund [Aspösund] and there are three islands of which one is Aspö, the other Refholm and the third Malmø [Nötö] and Iurima [Jurmo] is the most southerly nearest to the open sea.

Valdemar's Itinerary describes a route that nudges around south-western Finland and its southern coast, before leaving the land behind at Purkal (today's Porkkala, about ten miles east of what is now Helsinki) for the sea crossing to Tallinn. The place-names that match modern equivalents, and the many others that do not, suggest that the south-western islands and the area around Turku were sites of long-term human habitation, but the area of coast between the Hanko peninsula and what is now Helsinki would be depopulated and subsequently resettled, with only tenuous coastal trading posts and little permanent settlement inland.

In the 1290s, Torkel Knutsson seized the river-mouth sites of Vyborg and Kexholm (today's Priozersk on the shores of Lake Ladoga), fortifying them in old-fashioned Viking style with a fort on a river island. His decision was a matter of strategy and geography, since the two sites represented the two water courses of the Vuoksi river system. Whoever held Vyborg and Kexholm guarded the river route into Lake Saimaa, and hence the gateway to the Finnish hinterland.

But Torkel's occupation, of what had previously been Novgorod settlements, and (who knows?) maybe Swedish settlements once more before that, were not ratified until 1323, with the signature of a treaty between Sweden and Novgorod. It had no particular name at the time, but is usually known today as the Treaty of Nöteborg or Pähkinäsaari, the Swedish and Finnish names respectively for an island fort on the shore of Lake Ladoga. The treaty was not brokered by either side, but by exasperated Hanseatic merchants, sick of the unsure political situation in the area. At the urging of the Germans, the Swedes and Russians settled on a mutually agreed border, which roughly extended from the south-eastern corner of the Gulf of Finland, near the site of what is today St Petersburg, in a straight line to Oulu on the Baltic coast.

The Pähkinäsaari line established the cultural sphere of old Finland, although it barely encompasses a third of the country as we know it today. If the border were restored in modern times, it would exclude all of Lapland from Finnish authority, as well as Karelia and Kainuu – the towns of Kajaani, Iisalmi, and Kuhmo would be on the wrong side. It was only the southern end of the line that bothered the signatories, as it established a peaceful environment in the Vyborg area. The northern end was really of no concern to anyone, but established for the next 300 years the idea that the Karelia and Lapland areas remained wilderness, free for both Russians and Swedes to exploit.

People of the Österland

The Finns are phantoms throughout 600 years of Swedish history. One is often left wondering, when reading of 'Swedish' settlers in America, or 'Swedish' sailors encountered in foreign ports, to what extent the people described are actually Swedes from the Österland ('Eastland'), which is to say, Finns. As Swedish subjects, the Finns sent representatives to the election of kings, and soldiers to fight in Sweden's foreign wars.

During the Kalmar Union of 1397–1523, a series of chance dynastic coincidences and deals led the countries of Scandinavia to bond together under a single ruler. Denmark, Norway, and Sweden became a single realm, with Finland, as Sweden's easternmost marches, also included. The union also caused the administrative capital to move from Stockholm to Copenhagen, leaving the Finns further on the periphery. This isolation was accentuated during the Black Death, which killed off a third of the population of all Sweden, including the vulnerable homesteads of the remote Eastland. According to one eerie folktale everybody in the township of Espoo died except for a girl and a monk. When the monk, too, succumbed, the girl climbed the church tower and tolled the bell in his memory, signalling her presence to the only other survivor in the vicinity, her future husband.

Like an Adam and Eve of the borderlands, the couple became the ancestors of many future residents of Espoo, although much of the repopulation was arranged through royal decree, with boatloads of new settlers sent from the motherland. It is this phase, we might imagine, that is responsible for so many of the changes in place-names from those seen in *King Valdemar's Itinerary*.

After the break-up of the Kalmar Union, Finland became more prominent once more, as the Eastland of a Greater Sweden, which, at its height, straddled not only the north shores of the Baltic, but also extended south into what is now Estonia and Lithuania. This, in turn, involved the Finns indirectly in Sweden's many wars, as the master of the Baltic continued to jostle for influence against the Danes, the Russians, and the rising power of Germany.

The Pähkinäsaari line was often ignored. Despite the promise not to build castles along it, the Swedes put up several, including the impressive, still-standing Olaf's Castle in Savonlinna, named after that same Saint Olaf who, as a teenager, had raided the 'Balagard' coasts as a Viking. An entire community of trappers and hunters, the Pirkkalaiset, named for their original settlement in Pirkkala near Tampere, gained the right from the Swedish crown to fish in Lapland and collect tax from the locals – so the pacification of the borderlands was essentially farmed out to private industry, and woe betide any Russians who might run into them.

A minor issue of religion would prove to have lasting implications, when the dioceses of Uppsala and Turku established the line that marked the edges of their authority at Tornio, establishing a precedent for the boundary between 'Finland' and the rest of Sweden. Finland itself acquired greater influence during the fifteenth century, where its position as a marchland made it a crucible for forging future leaders.

Eric of Pomerania, King of all Scandinavia in the early 1400s, had spent his youth as the overlord of the Finnish border regions. Finland was a land with plenty of castles, and castles meant noblemen with armed retinues that needed to be appeased – turning many Finnish governors into members of the councils and king-making power blocs. In 1448, the Lord of Vyborg castle and former Lord of Turku was himself elected king, taking the throne as King Karl VIII (the first of three occasions, owing to the usual squabbling and politicking among the nobles of the time).

In 1523, the Reformation reached Finland in the figure of King Gustav I Vasa, who would see Catholicism ousted in his reign as Sweden's state religion, replaced by Lutheranism. This in turn would have far-reaching consequences, not least the translation of the Bible into Finnish by Mikael Agricola. Along with the same author's more modest but more immediately useful *ABC-kirja*, this not only taught Finns to read and write, but established the foundations of Finnish as a recognised language, and Finnishness as something separate from Sweden.

'Finlande is called a fayre Countrye, because it is more pleasanter than Swecia,' wrote George North in 1561, thereby making himself a hero evermore in the Finn–Swede standoff.

> Muche wyne is transported thither; out of Spayne,
> by the sea Balthic, which the people of the Country
> much desyreth, onely to exhillerat their myndes
> ... The Finnons have continual warres with the
> Muscouites in the arme or bosome of the sea
> Finnonicus: usyng in Summer the ayde of Shyppes,
> and in Wynter they combat upon the Ise.

According to popular lore in Europe, Finns were not only drunk, they were drunken wizards. Olaus Magnus, in his *Description of the Northern Peoples* in 1555, notes that there once was a time when:

> Finns, among other pagan delusions, would offer
> wind for sale to traders who were detained on their
> coasts by offshore gales, and when payment had
> been brought would give them in return three magic
> knots tied in a strap not likely to break.

Untying the first knot would rustle up a gentle breeze. The second would bring gusts sufficient to fill the sails of any ship. But the third would unleash hellish gales more likely to wreck the vessel than take it to a safe harbour. Olaus is swift to pour scorn on the very idea, offering an enlightened and curiously modern rant about gullible people's willingness to read rational outcomes into irrational claims. But the inhabitants of Lapland were regarded even into the sixteenth century as a people with magical powers. Olaus devotes several scornful chapters to the 'witches and wizards of the Finns', and when Shakespeare wishes to conjure up an image of bewitched confusion in *The Comedy of Errors* (1594), he notes: 'Lapland sorcerers inhabit here.'

Such authors' willingness to identify the people of the Arctic region as magicians owed something to their era. Both Olaus Magnus and Shakespeare were writing at a time when Lapland truly was the last frontier of European paganism. Although there had been earlier, sporadic exercises in preaching and conversion, missionaries only really arrived in force in the seventeenth and eighteenth centuries. With Christianity, of course, came a deep mistrust of pagan beliefs and ways of living – the purges and witch trials of the era saw the trampling of many folk traditions of medicine and belief. One of the most damaging acts of the missionaries in Lapland was the confiscation of shamanic drums from the priests of the Saami. The seat of a *noaidi* shaman's power, such drum-skins seem to have contained numerous mnemonic devices, symbolic summaries of rituals, and possibly even planisphere-like images of the constellations overhead. Pitifully few originals survive today, particularly since a misunderstanding over the missionaries' interest in the drums led to the manufacture of hundreds of fakes. During a period when earnest missionaries agreed to pay a small amnesty fee for any drums handed over, Saami in outlying regions commenced a cottage industry churning out new drums to exchange for cash. As a result, there is still some doubt as to the true provenance even of those supposedly genuine drums that can be found in Finnish museums.

By 1617, Lapland had been officially incorporated within the Swedish realm, after the treaty of Stolbova ended the seven-year Ingrian War, in which the Swedes had, as ever, attempted to push their borders further east. So, too, had Karelia, a region on the eastern marches where the local language was cognate with Finnish, but the local religion was overwhelmingly Russian Orthodox. Incoming Lutheran settlers were wary and dismissive of the Orthodox believers, who in turn regarded the new arrivals as *Saxa* ('Germans'). There were several attempts to institute a compulsory conversion of the Karelians to Lutheranism, gently but firmly refused by proclamation of the Swedish ruler, Queen Christina:

> The Royal Majesty does not find it right to use
> force against those who do not otherwise want to
> conform to persuasion nor to comply of their free
> will, nor the inquisition of a person's conscience.

Even so, there was a subtle but enduring campaign to ease the locals away from Orthodoxy, elements of which included a ban on the construction of new churches, the forbidding of conversions *to* Orthodoxy, and compulsory attendance at Lutheran Sunday services, whether someone was Lutheran or not. Such frictions eventually led to Russian intervention, with an invasion of Ingria and Kexholm in 1656, on the grounds that the Orthodox population needed to be defended – it also, handily, gained Russia access to strategic sea and river ports.

Although the Russian incursion was swatted away by 1658, the events soured the already tense relations in the region between Lutheran Swedes and Orthodox Karelians/Russians. Town records speak of parties and festivals that erupted into drunken brawls along sectarian lines, and disputes over land that ended in religious name-calling. By the 1670s, there were accusations from Lutherans that the 'Orthodox' Karelians were actually practising witchcraft, and that the secrecy and mistrust with which the Karelians often treated Lutheran investigations aimed to conceal forest orgies and ceremonies that denied Christ.

Reading through the accounts of alleged witchcraft, most seem to have been petty disputes and drunken confrontations, escalated along conveniently religious lines. There were, however, enough incidences of pagan ritual for the bishop of faraway Turku to observe that the remote communities were still in need of some Christian guidance:

> The peasants in this country practise great foolery with fishing, trailing and choosing extraordinary dates for holy days. When they get sick, they seek help from the Devil, sacrifice a thanksgiving for the Evil, carrying to the altar wax images, wax candles, squirrel skins, and other things ... They hand ox heads, calf heads and lamb heads on the walls of their houses and they converse with these in the dark so that no-one dares to own their God ...
> When they catch a bear, they organise a banquet in

the dark, drink a toast to the bear from its skull, and
growl like the bear growls to get more luck.

Local traditions took centuries to fade away. A hundred
years later, pastors would still be complaining about enduring folk beliefs, the use of pagan charms for luck and protection, secret divinations, burials in unhallowed ground,
and sundry other remnants of the old times. None of this
had anything to do with the Orthodox religion, which
remained a convenient scapegoat for certain Karelian
behaviours.

Finns in 'New Sweden'

As part of the colonisation, or often re-colonisation, of the
Eastland, Swedish settlers from Hälsingaland, 150 miles
north of Stockholm, arrived en masse to start a colony at
the mouth of the Vantaa River. Naming its first rapids for
their homeland, they called them the Helsingfors – the first
stirrings of what would ultimately become Helsinki.

Elsewhere, Finns formed a large and often silent part of
supposedly 'Swedish' ventures, not just at home but over-
seas. Of particular note here is the establishment in 1637
by the statesman Axel Oxenstierna of the New Sweden
Company, designed to take a Swedish presence to the New
World. The New Sweden Company was headed by a Finn,
Klaus Fleming, who wasted no time in leading two ships
across the Atlantic and dropping anchor in March 1638
on the Christina River in what is now Delaware. There,
after handing over some copper kettles, silver trinkets, and
various other items of junk, he claimed to have purchased

5,000 square miles of the west bank of the river from the local natives, stretching all the way from modern-day Wilmington to Pennsylvania. This, he announces, was New Sweden, which he left in the care of another Finn, Mauno Kling, while he went home to fetch some colonists.

The population of New Sweden comprised a mere twenty-three men for its early months, half of whom were Dutch in Swedish service. Nor was it all that successful, since Fleming returned home to discover that the animal pelts he had obtained on his mission had a market value back home of barely half the cost of the initial voyage. Undaunted, Fleming rounded up a number of colonists back home, many of whom would ultimately turn out to be Finns. Some, in fact, had already migrated once, from Finland to Sweden, where they had faced local antagonism over their unwelcome slash-and-burn farming methods. Jumping at the chance to get out of Sweden for somewhere more welcoming, they joined Fleming's scheme, many of them bringing their families, and subject to a contract that obliged them to work off the cost of their transport by performing two years of indentured labour.

With Finns forming at times up to 75% of the 'Swedish' colony in America, New Sweden struggled along until 1655, when it was peacefully occupied by the Dutch and ostensibly lost its connections to the motherland. In actuality this wasn't the case, since even under Dutch rule, it continued to attract settlers from Finland through the Netherlands, some of whom were found to be sneaking out of the country to Amsterdam in 1664, the same year that the 'Dutch' colony was itself seized by the British.

Five years later, a tall Finn by the name of Hendrick Kolman became one of the instigators of an attempt to overthrow the new rulers – an attempted insurrection by Finns, Swedes, and Dutch against the increasingly oppressive English. Whoever Kolman was, he had unwisely promised his conspirators that he would secure the support of the local Lenape Indians, being 'well verst in ye Indian language'. His co-conspirator, 'Königsmarke', went:

> ... up & downe from one place to another frequently raising speeches very seditious & false tending to ye disturbance of his Ma[jest]ies peace and ye Lawes of ye Govermnt.

The two men were soon apprehended, their schemes put to a swift end, although Kolman's sway with the Lenape was such that they appeared to have expressed an interest in starting a resistance of their own. They, unlike the rest of the local inhabitants, appeared to have fallen for his claims that a fleet of Swedish vessels was close at hand, and would soon arrive to seize back the land from the English.

For many years to come, the English rulers of America noted a certain surly and resentful character among the Delaware settlers, a ready resistance to tax collection and compulsory work levies, all of which they attributed to a character and attitude fostered by the attempted rebellion of 'the Long Fynne'.

As for the leader of the insurrection, despite the angry assertion by a New York court that 'the Long ffinne deserves to dye' he was instead sentenced to be 'publickly & severely whipt and stimatiz'd or Branded in the fface with the letter R with an Inscription written in great Letters and putt upon his Breast' announcing that he had been a would-be rebel, before being sold into slavery in Barbados.

In some circles, this 'Long Finn Rebellion' came to be thought of as the first stirrings of something greater. Almost a century later, on 1 July 1776, a deadlocked Congress would wait on the five members from Pennsylvania to decide on whether or not to declare independence from the British king. Two voted yes, two voted no, leaving the casting vote in the hands of one John Morton, whose grandfather, Martti Marttinen, had moved to America from Rautalampi, near modern-day Jyväskylä, Finland.

What would Morton say? At the deciding meeting the following day, the next thing out of his mouth would determine the very future. Was it time to stand up and declare a United States?

Morton rose to his feet, uttering a single word: 'Aye.'

Finland in the Northern Wars

Back in Europe, Sweden's 'Age of Greatness' included further wars over mastery of the Baltic, not only against Denmark, but also against the newly rising power of Poland, and ultimately in the Thirty Years War that engulfed almost all of the countries of Europe.

The 'Swedish' army in Europe included three regiments of light cavalry from Finland, from the Hämeenlinna, Turku, and Viipuri regions. They fought in many battles of the 1630s and 1640s, and were often known as the Hakkapeliitta, from their battle cry of *Hakkaa päälle!* ('Cut them down!' or more literally 'Strike on!'). To hear the Finns talk about them, you might be forgiven for thinking they were world-famous, but this seems to be a story that the Finns tell themselves, popularised by the works of Topelius (see Chapter 3), and reinforced in countless attempts by nineteenth-century schoolteachers to interest their classes in the complexities of the Thirty Years War. It was Topelius, in search of stirring narratives of the Finnish past, who popularised the 'Hakkapeliitta March' by translating the war-song of the seventeenth-century riders into Swedish. It remains on the repertoire of military bands in Sweden, Finland, and Germany, even though several of its verses amount to little more than bragging about places the singers have despoiled, and the people they've killed. The verses that sound slightly less like a party of rappers celebrating a drive-by shooting read as follows:

The snowy north is our fatherland;
There our hearth crackles on the stormy beach.
There our sinewy arm grew by the sword,
There our chests burned with faith and honour.
[...]
Take heart, you who dwell in darkness and chains!
We're coming, we're coming, we will free your hand.
Slaves do not sigh in our frosty North;
Freeborn we ride into the field for God's word.
[...]
And if we ride far from our northern track,
To glowing grenades and bleeding wounds,
East of Sweden: 1159–1809

Then the trumpets call the message of our victory.
Cut them down, brave ranks! Forward! With us is God.

The 'Hakkapeliitta March' sounds oddly old fashioned in the Finnish musical repertoire. Its tune is musically uninspiring; it is dwarfed and overshadowed by the stirring efforts of later composers like Sibelius. But the lyrics are nice enough, and the attention paid to them by Finnish educators has helped obscure the likelihood that nobody in Europe who heard the song ever actually understood the words, sung as they were in impenetrable Finnish.

Nor were the allies of the Hakkapeliitta all that sure who they were. One story of the Thirty Years War mentions a parade of soldiers, led by brightly attired mercenaries and hired swords, companies distinguished by flashes of regimental blue, yellow, or green. Bringing up the rear were nondescript cavalrymen on small, shaggy, fierce-looking ponies, with no notable uniform or brigade symbol, their trousers held up with string, and their horses bridled with chunks of birch-bark, their cutlasses dragging on the ground as if forgotten, their eyes stern and their cheeks hollowed.

The baffled Dutch ambassador asked what he was looking at, only for a German quartermaster to say he was looking at the Life Guards regiment. He then shouted '*Perkele!*', which he seems to have thought was their battle-cry, or possibly their regimental cheer. In fact, it is a Finnish swearword, presumably the only identifiable bit of Finnish he had ever heard from them, tantamount to the modern-day French observers who assumed that British football hooligans are called *les fuckoffs*.

The many wars and conflicts of the era found the Swedes jostling once more for supremacy in the Baltic, particularly against an even stronger Russia, as Novgorod was now absorbed within the larger princedom of Muscovy. Sweden met its match in the disastrous Battle of Poltava, in 1709, in what is now Ukraine. King Karl XII escaped, but spent the next five years in Moldavia, then part of the Ottoman Empire, pleading with his allies to lend him the money for a rematch. He would eventually return, bringing with him designs for two Ottoman-inspired warships, some new recipes (including *keftedes*, the distant ancestor of 'Swedish' meatballs, and *dolmades*, subsequently jury-rigged with cabbage leaves to make the *kaalikääryle*), and even some new vocabulary – a Swedish term for a disturbance, *kalabalik*, derives from the Turkish for 'crowd,' referring to the mobs of angry locals who descended on the growing camp of Swedish refugees.

In his absence, Finland suffered the years of the Great Wrath – occupation by the soldiers of Tsar Peter the Great. Thousands were killed, thousands more taken away as slaves, and a brutal scorched-earth policy pursued in order to create a barrier against Swedish counter-attacks. The Russians were gone by 1721, but only after the signature of the Treaty of Uusikaupunki, which cost Sweden much of the lands near Vyborg, and all its territory in and around Estonia. However, the change marked the end of Sweden's age as a great power, and the beginning of Russia's, while much of the damage was done, as usual, in Finland.

Sweden attempted to regain Vyborg in 1741, in a fool-hardily intricate scheme that was supposed to distract other countries from coups and skulduggery, but ended only with another defeat at the hands of the Russians. With the Swedish fleet paralysed by an epidemic of disease and unable to lend naval support to the attack, the Russians went on a swift counter-offensive, occupying Finland yet again in what is known as the Lesser Wrath. A treaty signed in Turku in 1743 would cost Sweden yet more territory, with the area around Lappeenranta and Hamina also handed to Russia.

With every treaty merely a temporary hiatus in hostilities, the Swedes prepared for another conflict, fortifying an island off the shore at Helsinki in the hope of making the city impregnable. The construction of this Fortress of the Swedes (*Sveaborg*), better known today as the Fortress of Finland (*Suomenlinna*) was witnessed in the 1780s by William Coxe, an English clergyman.

> The works are really stupendous and worthy of
> the ancient Romans. The walls are chiefly of hewn
> granite, covered with earth, from six to ten feet
> thick, and in a few places not less than 48 in height.
> The batteries, which begin upon a level with the
> water, and rise in tiers one above the other in all
> directions, commanding the only channel through
> which large vessels can sail to Helsingfors, render
> the passage of an enemy's fleet extremely dangerous,
> if not impracticable.

Despite all these awe-inspiring preparations, the fortress would not help. The final blow came in 1808, with a nineteen-month conflict between Sweden and Russia that would come to be known as the Finnish War, because Finland was the prize. Mired in the posturings and alliances of the Napoleonic conflict, it led to a Russian invasion of Finland without an official declaration of war, and the complete occupation of Finnish territory by winter 1808. In 1809, the nobles of Finland officially accepted that they had a new ruler, one who would hopefully not involve them in quite so many foreign wars. The Swedish era was over, with Finland's acceptance of the Russian Tsar Alexander I as its new head of state. In one of his early acts of generosity, he restored the lands of 'Old Finland' to the Grand Duchy, returning Vyborg and south-west Karelia to the Finnish state, in the interests of more streamlined management. The gift came at a price, with Finns expected to pay 'compensation' to the Russian nobles whose families had taken control of Old Finland a century earlier – a stipend that would continue to be extracted as late as the 1870s.

The Swedish Legacy

Linguistic evidence of the Swedish era endures in Finland, in everything from bilingual street signs to twinned subtitles in movie theatres. Finland's entire northern shoreline is named Ostrobothnia – which is to say, it is described as the east coast of the Gulf of Bothnia, rather than the more sensible 'west' Finland. South-west Finland, the rump around Turku, is still called Varsinais-Suomi ('Finland Proper'), a relic of the late medieval period when Swedish authority only really extended around the reach of Turku castle. A little north of there is Satakunta ('The Hundred'), an indicator of the slow extension of farms and authority.

The long stretch of southern coast from Turku to Helsinki is still called Uusimaa ('New Land'), a direct calque of the original Swedish Nyland, which was named for its status as a colony by royal decree, when the Swedish kings sent settlers to repopulate empty lands. And more immediately and importantly, all Finns still have to learn Swedish at school, although it is no longer a compulsory component of the high school matriculation exam. Swedish remains one of the country's two official languages, and is still the mother tongue of some 265,000 Finns (5.2% of the country). These are concentrated on the west and south coasts, historically the most 'Swedish' areas, where one can still often find street signs written in Swedish first and then Finnish. In particular, the Åland Islands, halfway between Finland and Sweden, are a Finnish possession but Swedish speaking.

This linguistic relic is often more visible to the tourist than to the resident, as any encounter with artefacts and figures from before the nineteenth century is sure to be heavily Swedish in nature – inscriptions, names, and fashions. There are statues of Swedish kings in the town centres of the Ostrobothnian coast, the food is often obviously Swedish in nature, and YLE Fem, the country's fifth TV channel, broadcasts in Swedish.

Throughout the early modern era, allegiance and connections to Sweden also signified a degree of old money and social standing, such that Swedish speakers formed all but three of Finland's noble families. Although modern Finland is bluntly, sometimes defensively egalitarian, any baron or count encountered in the history books is liable to have been a Swedish speaker. Swedish remained the default language of administration, the military, and education up until the later nineteenth century, in turn ensuring that anyone with a desire to truly understand the history of Finland must also learn Swedish. As late as 1894, Senator George Forsman caused gasps and uproar when he chose to address the Estate of Nobility in Finnish, instead of the Swedish lingua franca.

Wealth creates free time, and free time brings the greater likelihood of a career in the arts. This, in turn, favoured a Swedish-speaking bias among many of Finland's most famous creatives, including artists and writers before the nineteenth century, when Finnish nationalism began to assert itself in radical, vibrant, and enduring ways. With the Finnish language still struggling to develop modes and metres, clichés, and archetypes, many of the coming decades' assertions of Finnishness would be written first in Swedish.

But as the Finns were once ghosts in Sweden, the Swedes have become ghosts in Finland – a palpable presence along the west and south, but fading fast in the hinterland. You will hear their language in announcements on the train and bus; you will catch their weather forecasts; you will see tips of the hat to them in everything from street signs to flags, but they continue to dwindle, like the echoes of a lost age.

3

The Russian Century: 1809–1899

S enaatintori ('senate square') sits in the very heart of Helsinki, overlooking the harbour and its island fortress of Suomenlinna. It is flanked on all sides by institutions of authority – the great, classical columns of Helsinki Cathedral atop the steps on its north side; and the serried bookshelves of Helsinki University's main building on its west. On the eastern side is the former senate building, which now houses the Finnish prime minister and staff. On the south side is Sederholm House, the oldest mansion in Helsinki.

In the centre of the square stands a statue of a bushy-moustached man in the bulky epaulets and frog-tied tunic of a nineteenth-century general. But he stands at ease, his weight nonchalantly on his back foot, his right palm extended in a conciliatory fashion, as if he is making a friendly suggestion to an unseen audience. At his feet lurk a group of symbolic classical goddesses: Iustitia ('Justice'), wearing the pelt of a bear; Pax ('Peace') with her customary doves; and Lux ('Light/Enlightenment'), bearing a scientific instrument and accompanied by a lyre-playing cherub. With them are a gaggle of tough-looking peasants, representing honest labour.

The man who presides over this menagerie is Alexander

II (1818–81), the 'Good Tsar,' a figure loved so much by the Finns that his statue has endured in the centre of Helsinki throughout the conflicts of the twentieth century, including the Finnish Civil War, Stalinism, and the Cold War. He is captured here by the sculptor Walter Runeberg in a moment from 1863, in the act of re-convening the Diet of Finland, that body of local government that had not met since its leading noblemen had pledged their allegiance to their new Russian masters in 1809. Using the underpopulated Finland as an experimental test subject for potential reforms elsewhere in his empire, Alexander II bestowed upon it an element of home rule, its own currency (the markka, pegged initially as a quarter of the value of the Russian rouble), and a relaxation of the rules on using Russian in public institutions and records.

The statue is a glimpse of another bygone age – many modern Finns have grown up in a realm fiercely suspicious of Russia and Russians, and seem to have an ideological blind spot when it comes to the Tsar in the middle of their capital. But even after Alexander II's death, he remained a popular figure with the Finns, particularly as his heirs squandered his achievements. Throughout the reigns of his son, Alexander III, and ill-fated grandson, Nicholas II, the base of the statue would often be garlanded with flowers by reverent Finns. As the political climate turned increasingly frosty, Finns turned to the only means of subtle protest left to them, demonstrating their loyalty to Russia by honouring its ruler, but choosing to honour the ruler they loved the best, rather than his ham-fisted successors.

Even today, one sometimes finds flowers at the base of the statue, mourning a Russian love affair long turned sour.

Industrial Revolutions

The Russians were well aware that the people of the newly occupied territory occasionally chafed against the Swedes. The occupation hence began with a careful series of proclamations aimed at suggesting to the Finns that the Russians offered a better deal. The Diet, it was claimed (misleadingly), would still be convened. The Finns were free to practice their Lutheran faith, and the noble estates would be preserved. The message, then, was business as usual, with assurances of some degree of political autonomy, religious freedom, and no requisition of people's wealth. Many Finns greeted the news with little more than a shrug at the exchange of one unseen ruler for another.

'A defenceless country is like the sea,' commented one bishop pragmatically. 'Who is there to call it a sin if its waves roll up the shore the wind has driven them to? God has given us a ruler, and we must hold him up in honour.'

Russian troops were still skirmishing with Swedes elsewhere when the Tsar convened the Diet in Porvoo, March 1809. There, the nobility, as representatives of all Finns, swore allegiance to the Tsar, who whipped up a frenzy of unlikely hopes by commenting in his speech that the Finns had now been 'elevated to the family of nations'.

Timing was everything. Because the Finns had volunteered to accept Russian suzerainty *before* the Swedes had concluded peace, Finland's status was substantially higher than it might have been mere weeks later. Finland was never a conquered province of Russia, but instead an annexed Grand Duchy – the Tsar becoming its princely head of state.

The Russians were not particularly impressed with Finland. Since they already had trees, lakes, and snow of their own, the country initially had little to offer but a buffer zone between them and the rest of Europe, with limited transport and amenities, and thousands of square miles of wilderness and forest, stretching all the way to the Arctic.

'Boredom crawls over the snow wastes,' moaned the soldier Konstantin Batyushkov in 1809, 'and one can truly say that life in this wild barren solitude, without books, without company and often without aquavit is so miserable that we cannot tell whether it is Wednesday or Sunday.'

The French exile Madame de Staël was similarly dismissive on passing through in 1812, noting: 'They try to cultivate the mind a little there, but bears and wolves come so close in winter that all thought is of necessity concentrated on how to obtain a tolerable physical existence.'

By 1833, the prevailing opinion had changed little, with the poet Alexander Pushkin pronouncing Finland to be 'Nature's unhappy stepson', dealt all the pain of outdoors life, but with none of its pleasures. But Alexander II's reforms came accompanied by greater freedoms on foreign investment, and a new programme of railway-building that locked Finland closer to the Russian metropolis of St Petersburg. It should be said that this was much more important for the Finns than for the Russians, who had a whole empire to fret about, including ever-advancing tracts of land in the Siberian east. Consequently, despite the prominent position of Alexander II in Finnish history, Finland itself hardly gets a mention in Edvard Radzinsky's biography of the Tsar, barely warranting two index entries in a 450-page book.

The Russian era came accompanied by coincidental changes in technology and economy that were to the Finns' benefit. The industrial revolution elsewhere in Europe created an unexpected demand for Finnish wood and tar, which turned up as far afield as Britain, shoring up the roofs of coal pits and caulking ships of the line. Several British firms invested directly in Finnish lumber businesses, in order to ensure a steady supply. This in turn contributed to a rationalisation of water transport, with many of the scattered lakes linked by new canals. By 1856, it was possible to steam in a ship all the way from Viipuri on the Baltic coast to Kuopio, some 300 kilometres inland to the north.

Meanwhile, the exponential rise all over Europe of mass literacy and newsprint created a boom in the demand for paper, pouring money into the Finnish economy. Railways began arriving in the 1860s, with the early lines of the Finnish network connecting directly to St Petersburg in 1870. Although Finland had (and still has) remarkably few railway lines, those that it has have connected inland industrial areas to the sea ports since the late nineteenth century.

The Scottish missionary John Paterson spent much of the early eighteenth century in the Nordic countries. He was particularly taken with the rapids at Tampere, and inadvertently evangelised on the town's behalf. His posthumously published memoirs *The Book for Every Land* (1858) recount what happened when Paterson finally brought his friend James Finlayson face-to-face with the churning waters. Finlayson was less interested in natural beauty than in the implications of a twenty-metre drop in water height for setting up a mill.

> My friend Finlayson was delighted with the place. He at once perceived that I had not over-rated it in my description to him ... On our return to Petersburg, Mr Finlayson applied to Government for the grant of a small piece of land, on which to erect a manufactory for spinning cotton, and other purposes, and a sufficient command of water for the purpose. All and more than he asked was granted; and here works have been erected, which employ some hundreds of poor people, and being now entirely in the hands of pious men ... are a great blessing to the country ...

Although Finlayson had sold up and moved on within a few years, his name became synonymous with the six-storey factory he founded, the first in Finland to install electric lighting, and a powerhouse of the Industrial Revolution that led to Tampere's odd nickname, 'the Manchester of Finland'. Although Finland produced no raw cotton of its own, Alexander II's promise not to impose duty on Finlayson's imported materials remained good for the rest of the nineteenth century, and allowed the mills to become a centre for employment and development.

Steam tugs on the canals brought Russian tourists deeper into the lake land, but steam ships on the Baltic cut Finland off from many previous visitors. In the eighteenth century, many European travellers had regarded Finland as a necessary stop on the way to St Petersburg, making landfall at Turku and traversing the long coastal road along the Gulf of Finland. By the nineteenth century, steamship technology allowed any traveller in a hurry to board a vessel taking them straight to their destination, deleting Finland from many travellers' itineraries, but also ensuring that anyone who did go there was intent on enjoying it for its own sake, and not as something to stare at from the window of a post carriage. Finland became a place associated in the tourist's mind with wilderness and exotic Nordic open spaces, as best summed up by Ethel Brilliana 'Mrs Alec' Tweedie, the Victorian traveller whose journey around the country in the 1890s, *Through Finland in Carts*, remains an enchanting snapshot, both of Finns and of foreigners' perceptions of them.

No one ever dreamed of going to Finland.
Nevertheless, Finland is not the home of barbarians, as some folk then imagined; neither do Polar bears walk continually about the streets, nor reindeer pull sledges in summer – items that have several times been suggested to the writer. Few Finns noticed that the Tsar's reforms also lured them further away from their former masters in Sweden, encouraging trade links and travel to the east, rather than the west. Finns eventually became renowned as some of the most loyal and agreeable subjects of the Russian Empire, particularly in St Petersburg, where Finnish serving girls and sailors were common sights in the houses and taverns.

The same industrial revolution that put steamships into the Baltic also put smog into St Petersburg and anger into the hearts of the Russian working class. Travel restrictions on Tsarist Russians, designed to stop them learning unhelpful ideas like democracy and liberalism, led many of them to take their vacations in the only 'foreign' country within Russian authority, turning Finland's southern coast and eastern lakes into a vast Riviera of spa resorts and rural dachas. In particular, Terijoki (today's Zelenogorsk) became a veritable St Petersburg-on-sea, a bracing seaside resort for Russian holidaymakers, and notorious for occasional seafront brawls between drunken tourists. For the later Tsars, after the tragic assassination of Alexander II by Russian anarchists in 1881, Finland became a popular holiday destination *because* it was not Russia, and Finns could usually be counted on not to blow them up or shoot them while they were fishing or sunning themselves.

Laestadius & Laestadianism

Guarantees of religious freedom allowed the Protestant Lutherans to co-exist alongside the Eastern Orthodox Russians. Up in Lapland, the descendants of the Saami were facing increasing restrictions on their way of life. The Swedish enclosures of the late seventeenth century had not been reversed under Russian rule, leading to ever-encroaching homesteads and claims on what had once been deemed wilderness. Divisions and enclosures of land played havoc with Saami territorial concepts, particularly since many Saami tended to think in terms of access to water, rather than to the land around it. In an impasse bleakly familiar among many native peoples, the Saami were found to be in a long and precipitous decline into alcoholism and depression.

Lars Levi Laestadius (1800–61) was a pastor born into a Saami family in what was at least officially Swedish Lapland. Despite being of Saami ethnicity, and devoted to the cause of improving the conditions of his countrymen, he was also a super-devout Christian, determined not only to rescue the Saami from alcoholism, but to prevent them doing the Devil's work by whistling or calling to their reindeer with *joiks* ('songs').

Laestadius got his first parish posting in his late twenties, and spent the next twenty years preaching the gospel and administering to his flock in Karesuando – still technically in Sweden, but right on the Finnish border, on the 'wrist' of the map's Maid of Finland, and where the common tongue among the disparate herders and town-dwellers was Finnish. He fathered twelve children with his Saami wife, and functioned as a guide and botanist on a French academic expedition across Lapland, which would eventually result in his *Fragments of Lappish Mythology*, invaluable today as one of the only surviving accounts of the local folklore he was intent on stamping out.

In 1844, he first encountered a revivalist movement among the Saami that distinguished between true believers and 'false Christians'. Drawn by its fundamentalist principles and its inclusive, egalitarian practice that effectively rendered all true believers to be priests, able to hear confession from others, Laestadius fast became the leading light of the splinter group, which eventually took his name.

He eventually died in 1861, leaving his name nestled in the Latin designations of several Scandinavian plants, a temperance movement that would continue to grow throughout the latter part of the nineteenth century, and an Apostolic Lutheran sect that endures in isolated pockets in Finland, Scandinavia and those parts of the USA with a substantial population of Fenno-Scandinavian immigrants.

The most conservative of today's Laestadians, like the grimmest of Lutherans, Adventists, and similar revivalist denominations, continue to refer to themselves as 'true' believers, with the implication that everybody else is worshipping graven idols. Their services, as in the time of Laestadius, are lively and vibrant affairs, complete with sinners begging their fellows for forgiveness. Of the world's 115,000 conservative Laestadians (the splinter group having further splintered) most are to be found in modern Finland where their existence is unlikely to reach the notice of the average tourist. Their presence becomes decidedly more palpable for anyone who has raised a child in Finland, as Laestadian families tend to be noticeable at day-care and schools. Shunning contraception, they tend to the larger size, particularly when their insistence of no sex before marriage incentivises couples to get married as soon as possible.

Hence, it is not unusual to run into a married couple in their late twenties with five children, nourished and well-kept by the Finnish welfare system, and often impeccably well behaved, thanks to the Laestadians' hatred of television and cinemas. This latter proscription, however, is being eroded in many Laestadian homes, as rules-lawyers insist that the internet 'doesn't count' as TV, and therefore everyone can huddle around the computer to watch the latest sinful episode of *The Amazing Race*.

The Great Migration

As a critical component of Russia's navy and merchant marine, Finns were often at the forefront of the empire's further conquests. It was Adolf Erik Nordenskiöld, born in Helsinki, who first navigated the Northeast Passage across the top of Asia, and who explored the Greenland ice sheet in the company of Saami skiers. Finns also spear-headed the march of Russia across the Bering Strait and into Alaska, which was a Russian colony until it was sold off to the United States in 1867. The penultimate governor of Russian Alaska was himself a Finn, Johann Furuhjelm, appointed to the post after service in the Russian–American company that had seen him sail to Hawaii, California, and China, and even command a ship as part of an ill-starred 1850s mission to the closed country of Japan.

As Russia rolled back its ambitions from the New World, the Tsar pinned his hopes instead on the Amur River basin, a sprawling, swastika-shaped confluence of rivers in north-east Asia that he hoped would prove to be a 'new Mississippi' in the Russian Far East. You can still find faint traces of the Russian dream of an Asian utopia, such as in what is now a district in the Finnish industrial town of Tampere. Built in the 1860s as affordable wooden housing for factory workers, it took its name from what was then the most remote and promising river outpost of the Russian empire, *Amuri*.

The 1860s were a time of great deprivation and famine

in Finland, leading the Tsar to make many Finns an offer they could not resist – freedom to settle in a new land of promise, out beyond the Amur River on the coast of Siberia, in 'Outer Manchuria'. Many Finns took up the Tsar on his offer, including the fantastically named Fridolf Fabian Höök, a sea captain who led several ill-fated colonisation missions in the Far East. The Amur did not prove to be as navigable as the Russians had hoped, and the likes of Captain Höök faced marauding Manchurian bandits and harsh winters. Before long, the only enduring evidence of their presence was a naval base a little to the south, originally named for the Finnish-Swede who first discovered it, as Jägerskiöld's Town, but eventually rechristened 'Domination of the Orient' (*Vladivostok*). Some years later, it would become the terminus of the game-changing Trans–Siberian Railway.

Finns also formed a substantial community among the gold miners who moved to Victoria, Australia in the 1850s. But it was to the United States of America and Canada that Finnish emigrants truly flocked in what became known as the Great Migration. Finns emigrated in their thousands, not along the perilous eastward route towards Siberia, but westward, through Europe, towards the American Midwest. Throughout the late nineteenth century, increasing numbers of Finns ignored the Russian incentives and instead took offers from America for copious work opportunities as home-steaders, miners, and loggers in the United States.

To America, to America,
That's where everyone is bound

Sand of gold covers the ground
On the road to America.

Many of the Finns who went to America never intended
to stay, merely to save up enough money in order to return
home again and buy land or set up a business of their own.
As prospects continued to look better in America than back
home, some settlements turned into permanent Finnish
enclaves. Within Minnesota, in particular, in Michigan's
Upper Peninsula, and across Lake Superior in Canada's
Thunder Bay, the Finnish-speaking population grew so
large that it exerted a gravitational force of its own on new
migrants and long-term cultural artefacts. Sometimes, this
was as simple as place-names and amenities with a clear
Finnish origin, like Hancock, Michigan, with its Finlandia
University and its Suomikatu ('Finland Street'), or Minnesota towns named for the *Kalevala*, distant homes like Savo
or Waasa (this last retaining an archaic W from what is now
Vaasa), or Finnish words, like Toivola ('Hopeville'), Wuori
('Fell') and Salo ('Backwoods').

For a hundred years, Finns all over the homeland cherished memories of, or aspirations to visit, relatives in the land
they called *Amerikka* – the doubled consonantal ending
offering an almost Hispanic flourish to the sound, like
something out of *West Side Story*. Meanwhile, for Finnish-
Americans, the golden rule of cultural assimilation – that it's
the third generation that loses the former mother tongue –
was postponed and kited for decades, fed by local Finnish-
language newspapers and amateur dramatic societies, and
a local publishing niche that clung quaintly to old-world

vocabulary. Second generation Finnish-Americans kept up their language skills by working as waitresses in Finnish-speaking canteens, or alongside newly arrived miners from Europe. The linguistic polder kept many Finns in lower-ranking jobs, resentful of Cornish or Irish miners promoted more swiftly up the ladder because they spoke English. The poet Kalle Koski wrote in 1894 about the dangers of racial mixing, conjuring the image of a Finnish girl who falls for a *wieras airis*, a beautifully archaic clash of old-world spelling and migrant slang – 'a foreign Irish'. Such cross-cultural romances bred new and alien phenomena, such as Finnish Catholics, a great rarity back in Europe, where the Reformation had seen Catholicism hounded from the country centuries earlier. Even today, Michigan's Upper Peninsula has a Finnish ethnic component of an estimated 16%, and even had its own Finnish-language television programme, *Finland Calling*, until 2015.

The Åland War

In 1853 the outbreak of the Crimean War pitted the Tsar's Russian Empire, including the Grand Duchy of Finland, against an international coalition including the fading might of the Ottoman Empire, shored up by its British and French allies. Much of the fighting, of course, was in Crimea itself, but the conflict also led to skirmishes as far afield as Kamchatka and Sardinia. Much overlooked in histories of the Crimean War is the two-year campaign in the Baltic Sea, where an Anglo–French taskforce shelled the edges of the Russian Empire, and bottled the Tsar's fleet in St Petersburg. Most crucially, the Tsar's constant fear of an attack on

St Petersburg itself led him to keep 30,000 Russian soldiers stationed close at hand, thereby keeping them away from the main theatre.

Despite this contribution, the actions of the British in the Baltic have been mainly forgotten. Admirals get famous for sinking ships, not simply keeping their enemy distracted and setting fire to the tar silos. Moreover, the Baltic action was also something of an embarrassment, since on several occasions attempted British landings were thwarted by simple geographical hazards and a population of bullish locals. At least one Finnish coastal town, Kokkola, still talks proudly of the dead English sailors in its graveyard, and has yet to return the gunboat that unwisely attacked it.

The allies' greatest success was the destruction of Bomarsund, a recently constructed Russian sea-fort overlooking the strategic harbour in the middle of the Åland Islands. Less successful were several assaults on Helsinki's off-shore fortress Sveaborg (better known today by its Finnish name, Suomenlinna), the cause of much finger-pointing. The admiral on site was convinced that Sveaborg was unassailable without a particular kind of low-draft mortar-launcher that he lacked; armchair generals back home were equally sure that he simply lacked the courage or intelligence to carry out his orders.

The worst long-term effect of the Baltic campaign was the damage to the reputation of the 'English' among the Finns, who had long cherished the notion of a special affinity with the nation that had, after all, supplied their patron saint. This was not lost even back in Britain, where questions were asked in Parliament about the wisdom of carrying out a war against Russia by attacking defenceless Finnish villagers, and burning the tar warehouses of Oulu and Raahe.

More than 150 years after the Baltic campaign, it is still a recurring museum feature all along the coast of Finland, where despite the modern might of the steam navy, the skerries and shallows often reduced the attackers' presence to humble rowboats and landing parties that were considerably more vulnerable than the warships that launched them.

A song, purportedly celebrating the defence of the Åland Islands, has entered the modern Finnish military repertoire, despite its best-known version's careful avoidance of mentioning that the Finns actually surrendered. Here is part of it:

Oh the Åland War was horrific
Hurrah! Hurrah! Hurrah!
When on three hundred ships
Came the Englishmen sailing to our Finnish coast
Sunfaraa Sunfaraa Sunfaralalala
Hurrah! Hurrah! Hurrah!
[...]
But the Finnish boys fired at them
Hurrah! Hurrah! Hurrah!
Echoing round the walls of the island fastness
Ringing on the Åland shores
Sunfaraa Sunfaraa Sunfaralalala
Hurrah! Hurrah! Hurrah!

'Oolannin Sota' ('the Åland War') is a stirring toe-tapper, sure to be dragged out at military occasions, which, in a country that still has national service, is liable to involve almost everybody's family at some point in their lives. It also seems particularly popular with Finnish maiden aunts who wish to torment British authors by singing it constantly to their half-Finnish children while babysitting – many are the times, when writing this book, that your correspondent has been assailed by 'Hurrahs' from downstairs.

The problem with 'Oolannin Sota' is that it appears to have sprung up out of nowhere; it is unknown on the Åland Islands themselves, where the claim that the local beaches amounted to 'our Finnish coast' would be regarded by many of the Swedish-speaking locals as somewhat provocative.

It was included in an early book of Finnish military music in 1918, but no song with that title pre-dating 1910 has been unearthed. As one might expect from a song purported to come from the Åland Islands, the language of the song is heavily peppered with actual Swedish words, although the first extant version of it in Swedish is a translation from what appears to be the 'original' Finnish.

It was not until 1975 that a musicologist found a nineteenth-century edition of the similarly named 'Ålandin Sota', a close match in melodic terms, but with substantially different words. While the version most widely known and sung is an exuberant, triumphal celebration of the brave Finns repulsing the hapless Englishmen, the song uncovered by Kalevi Ijäs in a remote mainland farm is a far more honest account of the destruction of Bomarsund. It appears that the original version of 'Ålandin Sota' may have been written by one Johan Wallenius, a Finnish prisoner of war from Bomarsund, who sat out the last months of the conflict along with several hundred other Finns in the East Sussex town of Lewes.

The 'Russian' prisoners of war in Lewes are commemorated by a stone obelisk that still stands in the local churchyard of St John sub Castro. Commissioned by Tsar Alexander II, the memorial records the names of twenty-eight 'Russians' who died during their incarceration – the names are almost universally those of Finnish conscripts, rather than their Russian officers.

Their surviving fellow inmates became local celebrities in the town, regarded as exotic foreign curios, and put to work on what proved to be a lucrative carpentry business making 'Russian' toys for sale to local children.

It seems that while languishing in relative luxury in Lewes' Old Gaol, the prisoners wrote the original version of the song, quite possibly adding new verses as their own story went on, resulting in a version much longer than the one sung today, with eighteen verses penned in an odd patois of half-remembered Swedish and misspelt Finnish – as if illiterate Ostrobothnian farmboys were attempting to remember officers' terms they had never correctly heard in the first place.

Their account tells of the war coming to the Ålands, and of the 'Finnish boys' shipped over from the mainland to prepare for their defence. 'Two hundred' ships arrive in this version, crewed with greater historical accuracy by both French and Englishmen (the terms mangled almost childishly into *franskalaine* and *engetesman*). There is an attack, there is a command given in haste, and then some accusatory verses about the unnecessary deaths this causes. The 'flag of grace' is raised in surrender, and the Finnish boys are marched away to an uncertain fate. They live for 'a year and eight months in the English kingdom' before being allowed to return home.

Then came the command from the Emperor
Hurrah! Hurrah! Hurrah!
That allows the captured boys and their father back to
    their land.
Sunka fralla [a mangled version of the Swedish for
    'Sing tralala']
So the boys they cheered and shouted
Hurrah! Hurrah! Hurrah!
And said their farewells through the town of Leves [sic],
As they stepped down to their white/fire ship
Sunka fralla
And the boys sang in the harbour
Hurrah! Hurrah! Hurrah!
That the English kingdom was wonderful
But our fatherland is yet more marvellous
Sunka fralla

Translating even the basic sense of it is difficult, when one can see that the authors meant one word, but only because they had misheard another. There may have even been multiple versions of a collectively written song, diverging into one form in which the Finns return home in a *valki-alaiva* (strangely poetic, but presumably a steam ship), and another in which the Finns leave in a *tulivaunu* (a 'chariot of fire', possibly referring to the twenty-eight prisoners who died, or possibly a sweetly clueless reference to a steam train). It remains an odd, indistinct echo of real lives catapulted from the shores of Finland to the English coast, and home again, one-and-a-half centuries ago.

The Kalevala

It was during the Russian century that Elias Lönnrot (1802–1884), a physician and folklorist, collected a different sort of song in the wilds of Karelia. Posted to the remote town of Kajaani for much of his career, Lönnrot busied himself by taking prolonged journeys into the eastern lands, collecting and collating songs and stories from local storytellers – ironically, many of those same pagan traditions that the authorities had spent centuries trying to wipe out. Where once they had been embarrassing throwbacks, the folk beliefs of Karelia now became a fount of Finnish identity.

Lönnrot's aim, among the peasants of the remote communities, was to dig up specifically Finnish folktales that might have endured in the hinterland even as they were wiped out by the onslaught of Swedish and Russian culture in the towns. Adding bridging material of his own, Lönnrot fashioned the disparate stories into a single song cycle, publishing it as the *Kalevala*, Finland's national epic.

The cycle of stories, as eventually set down by Lönnrot, presents a creation myth and series of epic conflicts among the forests and lakes of an ancient Finland. It remains charmingly modest in its aspirations, and its depiction of a relatively simple life in the forests – it has no fairytale castles, and the ancient gods of Finland take a back seat. Instead, it is preoccupied with the bickering and feuds of a bunch of heroes, rich with detail about daily life and material culture in the Finnish Dark Ages.

Although the gods are occasionally present, the stories of the *Kalevala* dwell for most of the time on the heroes, particularly 'steadfast, old Väinämöinen', the first man. We see him born to the goddess Ilmatar, and instrumental in the creation of many elements of the Finnish natural world and ancient society.

Väinämöinen is already an old man when he encounters and duels with the hero Joukahainen, who promises him his sister Aino as a bride if he spares his life. Väinämöinen agrees, only for Aino to drown herself in a lake. Several stories then follow in which these heroes are presented as long-suffering woodsmen, toiling in a series of herculean labours in the hope of winning the hand of another fair maiden. In particular, several heroes chase after the daughters of Louhi, the shapeshifting queen of the northern land of Pohjola. Väinämöinen persuades the master-smith Ilmarinen to create the Sampo, a magical device of indeterminate function that may have once been a magical shield, or icon or symbol. Lönnrot's version suggests it is a machine or cornucopia, part forge and part mill.

On one side the flour is grinding,
On another salt is making,
On a third is money forging,
And the lid is many-colored.
Well the Sampo grinds when finished,

To and fro the lid in rocking,
Grinds one measure at the day-break,
Grinds a measure fit for eating,
Grinds a second for the market,
Grinds a third one for the store-house.

Whatever it is, and much ink has been spilled over it ever since, it soon turns into a MacGuffin over which everybody is fighting. Louhi sets a number of impossible tasks for the heroes who want to marry her daughters. The hero Lemminkäinen dies attempting such missions, but is raised from the dead by his sorcerous mother. Ilmarinen the smith actually completes his tasks, with the help of the Maiden of the North, who is sweet on him. The result is the wedding to end all weddings, in which there is much celebration and heroic guests provide ostentatious gifts and food – all except for Lemminkäinen, who is not invited, and stomps off sulkily to have a series of adventures on his own.

But there is no happy-ever-after for Ilmarinen and his new wife. She picks on the wrong slave, a troubled orphan called Kullervo, whose difficult early life forms a separate, ominous story cycle, not unlike a flashback in which someone discovers that the person whose seat he just stole on the train is actually Hannibal Lecter. Kullervo sees his mistress dead at the claws of a gang of wolves and bears, and then runs off to avenge his family, starting a war and inadvertently having sex with his sister, before killing himself in grief.

Single once more, Ilmarinen attempts to make himself a woman out of gold and silver, but finds her unsurprisingly emotionless. Instead, he heads off back to the north to snatch another of Louhi's daughters, leaving in a hurry after having turned the angry Louhi into a bird. Back in the south, he tells Väinämöinen of the wealth that the Sampo has brought to Louhi's people, and the heroes head off to steal it. In the massive, sorcerous apocalypse that follows, armies of men are slaughtered on both sides, as the combatants war with steel, ships, and magical songs. The Sampo falls into the ocean while set in its condiment mode, and is still somewhere at the bottom, endlessly churning out salt. The vengeful Louhi orders a series of plagues on the south, and the heroes fight back with a prolonged series of magical solutions and damage controls.

Finally, as discussed in Chapter 1, a virgin called Marjatta gives birth to a baby boy, having become pregnant by eating a berry. Väinämöinen orders it to be killed, but the child scolds him and is baptised as the King of Karelia. Realising that the time of the old beliefs has passed, Väinämöinen leaves his realm in the hands of the Christ-figure, and sails away.

National Romanticism

The *Kalevala*'s impact was immense. Among European literati, it became a subject of great debate, since Lönnrot had seemingly uncovered an epic worthy of comparison to Greek and Roman classics among illiterate peasants at the edge of the known world. It was also seized upon as a work of inspiring nationalism, arguing, in the fashion of the Brothers Grimm, that a people who had a story and a language also had the right to a nation. As a truly national myth, divorced from associations with either Sweden or

Russia, the *Kalevala* was also seized upon by a generation of Finnish artists in search of 'Finnish' subjects.

Aleksis Kivi (1834–72) chose the *Kalevala* as the source of his first play, writing the tragedy *Kullervo* in 1864 and initiating the medium of Finnish-language theatre. Finnish painters, particularly Akseli Gallen-Kallela (1865–1931) rushed to depict *Kalevala* subjects, enriching Finnish artistic life with images divorced from the previous dominant cultures of Sweden and Russia – the tragedy of Aino, the vengeance of Kullervo, and the theft of the Sampo. Many of these are bombastic propaganda images of rage, melancholy, and action. Others are beautifully subtle, such as the four paintings Gallen-Kallela made of Lake Keitele in central Finland, criss-crossed with wind-blown ripples ... Perhaps the wake of Väinämöinen's boat, just out of the edge of the frame, gone, but not forgotten?

Within only a few years, *Kalevala* subjects were highly visible, in frescoes, woodcuts, and statues, injecting a powerful and unprecedented presence of Finnishness into the evolving critical conversation about art and life. Just as enduringly, the *Kalevala* also became something that could be heard, when the composer Johan 'Jean' Sibelius (1865–1957) began writing symphonies and tone poems on subjects including Kullervo and Lemminkäinen. The period of the *Kalevala*'s greatest flourishing as a theme, the 1890s, coincided with the rise of the arts and design movement known in Britain as Art Nouveau, and in Finland by its German title, *Jugendstil*. This, in turn, led to the peppering of central Helsinki with glorious cod-medieval follies – hotels, restaurants, and offices built like castles and chased with carvings, frescoes, and motifs drawn from Lönnrot's song cycle, as if the buildings themselves are auditioning for a walk-on role in *Game of Thrones*.

Playing 'I-Spy' with *Kalevala* references can keep the visitor to modern Finland busy for days. It is not merely a case of street names and districts, statues, and paintings, it leaps out at you in the supermarket and at the bank. Little rye biscuits are called Väinämöinen's Buttons. Pohjola, home of the money-making Sampo, is the name of a Finnish bank, as was Sampo itself until recently. Children from good Christian families are baptised with the names of pagan gods and heroes – it is normal to run into a boy called Tapio, after a Finnish forest god, or a girl called Aino, presumably named for the character's legendary beauty rather than her suicidal depression.

The *Kalevala* also influenced foreign writers. *Hiawatha* lifts much of the meter from its German edition, while the young JRR Tolkien was deeply moved not only by its stories, but by the idea that they had been reconstructed from the relics of a pre-Christian past. In his twenties, he attempted to write his own version of the *Kalevala*'s story of Kullervo, although his take on the legend was shamelessly Anglo-Saxon in its meter and tone. You can almost imagine a much older Tolkien, chuffing on his pipe by a fireside, and beginning with *Jackanory* cadences:

> In the days when magic was yet new, a swan
> nurtured her brood of signets by the banks of a
> smooth river in the reedy marshland of Sutse. One
> day, as she was sailing among the sedge-fenced pools

with her trail of younglings following, an eagle
swooped from heaven and flying high bore off one
of her children to Telea ...

This is all very well, but it is a far cry from the primal, recursive, repetitive song-talk of the original, which is faintly preserved even in the old 1888 *Kullervo* translation by John Martin Crawford. Your mileage may vary, but for *Kullervo* to really hit the right note with me, it needs to sound more like this:

In the ancient times a mother
Hatched and raised some swans and chickens,
Placed the chickens in the brushwood,
Placed her swans upon the river;
Came an eagle, hawk, and falcon,
Scattered all her swans and chickens ...

The original literally lacks the vocabulary to avoid repeating itself. It is a spiralling cycle, intended not to be read but to be *performed*, constantly looking over its shoulder to make sure that the audience is keeping up.

Tolkien's version turns it into a narrative story with an occasional song interlude. He buffs it up for a notional audience of hobbits – as we might expect, he is already working through a nascent idea for a similar invented tradition of the English. Years later, he would hammer together his own pseudo-mythology, positing an epic quest of demigods and heroes to forge and retain mythic magic jewels called *silmarils* (Finnish: *silmä* is 'eye'). Tolkien created a language for his elves, Quenya, derived from Finnish itself. His love affair with the *Kalevala*, first mentioned in a letter to his fiancée as early as 1914, would eventually evolve into *The Lord of the Rings*.

Tolkien never visited Finland, but wrote movingly of the powerful sense of it that was imparted by Lönnrot's work. Spend too much time on the *Kalevala*, he wrote, and:

> Trees will group differently on the horizon, the birds will make unfamiliar music; the inhabitants will talk a wild and at first unintelligible lingo. I hope ... after this the country and its manners have become more familiar, and you have got on speaking terms with the natives, you will find it rather jolly to live with this strange people and these new gods awhile, with this race of unhypocritical scandalous heroes and sadly unsentimental lovers: and at the last, you may feel you do not want to go back home for a long while if at all.

However, not all is as it seems. Some might argue that the national myth of the *Kalevala* is itself something of a myth. There was, and remains, some debate as to how much of the *Kalevala* is genuine forensic anthropology of ancient folktales, and how much of it was finessed and filtered by Lönnrot himself – Juha Pentikäinen's book *Kalevala Mythology* points to some persuasive parallels between certain events in Lönnrot's own life and key moments in his song cycle. Derek Fewster, in his study of Finnish nationalism *Visions of Past Glory*, notes that while the *Kalevala* undoubtedly made an impression on certain sectors of the artistic community, the way its stories reached the general population was often second- or third-hand. The modern-day visitor to Finland is apt to believe that the *Kalevala* transformed the entire nation in an ecstasy of reading and response, whereas it had barely sold 130,000 copies by 1937. Instead, the most influential work in creating Finnishness was the *Book of Our Country*, published in Swedish in 1875 and Finnish a year later, by the author Zacharias Topelius. Topelius easily topped 340,000 sales in dual languages by 1908, becoming a school textbook, and hence the first point of contact that many Finns had with notions of Finnishness.

Intended for younger readers, Topelius toned down the sex and violence of other accounts of Finnishness. He was also apt to repeat ideas from some of his earlier works, when, as a younger man, he had written a somewhat Sweden-centric account of Finnish history. Like earlier Norse authors, Topelius was slippery in his use of the term 'Finn', sometimes referring to Saami, sometimes to Suomi, sometimes to scattered tribes that might one day make up Finnish ethnicity. 'Finnishness' was often parsed as an absence or an ignorance – the primitive, savage tribes of the Eastern Land, succumbing with great reluctance to the light of Swedish culture and Christian belief.

As a result, much of the nineteenth-century dialogue about the nature of Finnishness had to pull the concept up by its bootstraps, out of nothingness. Was there a Finnish 'kingdom' before the arrival of the Swedes? Since the Finnish language seemed to lack a native word for 'king', probably not. But what if the ancient legends of Finnish gods and heroes were actually garbled references to actual human beings? If the heroes of the *Kalevala* were once real people, and those people once led men and took wives, then surely that would point to an edifice of Finnishness?

What about religion? The Finns, according to all the Swedish records, were the savage barbarians who were forced at the point of a sword to convert to Christianity. So perhaps we might see Finnishness in Lalli, the murderer of St Henry? Maybe Finnishness can be reconstituted in opposition to St Henry's Catholic religion, by making a sign of true Finnishness to be the later, enthusiastic adoption of the more modern, Lutheran faith?

The academic and polemicist Johan Vilhelm Snellman (1806–81) saw Finnishness as inherent in the language itself, and wrote articles, in Swedish, urging the upper classes of Finland to begin using the language of the Finnish majority in their daily life. Finnish grew in use in schools, and also in people's names, as Swedish speakers marked their allegiance to a sense of Finnishness by 'Fennicising' their names, often directly translating the meaning of their Swedish surname into its Finnish equivalent. For example, Aleksis Kivi, the author, had previously been Alexis Stenvall. Aleksi Gallen-Kallela had begun his life as the plainer Axel Gallén. Kaarlo Ståhlberg, later Finland's first president, had been Carl Ståhlberg before the movement.

The search for Finnishness became of greater importance towards the end of the nineteenth century, when Russia's benign policies towards the Grand Duchy became increasingly proscriptive, and the Finns began to push back.

4

A Nation is Born: 1899–1939

Finland is festooned with statues of Carl Gustaf Mannerheim (1867–1951). Today his effigy walks with a
jaunty step in the central town square of Mikkeli, where
his statue was controversially moved after spending the
Cold War somewhere less visible; as it were, only having
his victory parade when the coast was clear. He walks his
horse unheedingly past the Finnish parliament building
on the Helsinki street that bears his name; a rival equestrian design trots insolently outside Lahti train station. He
lurks a little hesitantly in a Seinäjoki park, and there's even a
bust of him right here in my Jyväskylä office. But Tampere's
Mannerheim statue is very different, tucked away in a forest
on a hilltop on the outskirts of the town. A notice beneath
the statue reads that it was 'from this hill' that Mannerheim
looked down at the Battle of Tampere in 1918. It neglects to
add that the statue was originally commissioned to stand in
the centre of Tampere, but events conspired against it.

The original idea came on the twentieth anniversary of
the Battle of Tampere, when the rich local industrialist and
former council leader Rafael Haarla proposed a monument
to the leader of the 'Whites'. It was already a confronta-
tional move – as a member of the ruling class and a sup-
porter of the anti-Communist Whites, Haarla had been

stabbed and assaulted in 1918, and was determined to ram home the message that his side had prevailed. He died in 1938, but the project to build the statue went ahead, despite the objections of Mannerheim himself, who really didn't like the idea of being commemorated before he was dead.

The Second World War led to the postponement of the plans, and by the time the dust had settled, Tampere's council had swung far to the left. Mannerheim was, by that time, a different kind of national hero (see Chapter 5), but the Tampere statue was blatantly provocative, aping the clothes and pose of a famous portrait of White Mannerheim from 1918, not the defiant Marshal of Finland of 1939. Horrified that they had inherited a giant bronze image of the man who had rounded up Finland's Reds, the socialist council prevaricated for a while, and then decided on a compromise, siting the statue of their nemesis out in the sticks. Perhaps, in itself, this was a commentary on Mannerheim's role in the Battle of Tampere, subtly suggesting that he should have come a bit closer to the town in order to see what was being done there in his name.

The original intended base of the Mannerheim statue now hosts a memorial to the White soldiers. The original intended site is occupied by a shepherd-boy nude, flanked by a couple of sheep, commemorating the 150th anniversary of a local cotton mill. Mannerheim, on the other hand, stares down at the city he once attacked. In 2004, he was voted the greatest Finn of all time in a national TV survey. The next day, someone daubed a single word in red paint across the base of his statue: *Lahtari* ('Butcher').

Russification

The Russian honeymoon began to fade by the 1880s. The growing power of Bismarck's Germany, and the growing unrest within the Tsar's Empire itself, placed the ruler under stronger pressure to bring Finland more firmly into the fold. There were already signs in the 1880s that the growing Finnish nationalist movement faced stronger opposition in the government of its Grand Prince, but the real effects did not begin to show until the death of Alexander III in 1894.

He was succeeded by his son, Nicholas II, remembered today as the last of the Romanovs, but better known in Finland as 'The Perjurer' for what is perceived to be his betrayal of the Tsar's traditional oath to uphold Finnish autonomy. In 1899, Nicholas produced the stern, unequivocal February Manifesto, announcing that from now on, only roubles would be legal tender in Finland. The Finnish post office would now use Russian stamps, and the official religion of state was now the Orthodox Church.

Nicholas followed this in 1900 with a Language Manifesto that decreed Russian to be the official language of administration. A year later, he signed a Conscription Law that effectively abolished the Finnish army, obliging Finns instead to join up in the Russian military, where the language of administration was also Russian. With only 8,000 Russians in the Grand Duchy, 2.5 million Finns were effectively relegated to second-class citizens, unless they could learn the language of their masters.

In Finland, these reforms were regarded as a coup d'état, wiping out decades of promises and goodwill made to the supposedly autonomous Finns by successive Tsars. Nor was it possible to protest quite so freely as before, since the press was now subject to a Russian censor.

'We have found it necessary to reserve to Ourselves the final decision,' wrote Nicholas, 'as to which laws come within the scope of general imperial legislation.' Or in other words, every single scrap of freedom permitted to the Finns since 1809 was merely at the sufferance of the Tsar; freedoms were only leased, not permanently granted.

In 1898, Nicholas had appointed a new figure to implement these measures, his hatchet-man Governor-General Nikolai Bobrikov, an aging military officer who looked like Ming the Merciless with pince-nez spectacles. Bobrikov is remembered by the Finns as an awful despot, although Russian accounts present him as a driven, loyal man, determined to do the right thing by his Tsar, working all hours and weakened by a series of heart attacks. He arrived in Finland to conduct a brief inspection tour, and came away distinctly unimpressed.

'Everything proved that Finland has nothing in common with the Empire,' Bobrikov observed. 'I felt as if I were travelling in a foreign country. And this is the closest borderland to the Empire's capital, a region which is strategically very important.'

Bobrikov tightened the Tsar's hold even further, decreeing that the number of school lessons taught in Russian should be increased, and demanding that all correspondence between institutions also be in Russian.

The Finns fought back in a number of protests, a reassertion of a 'Fenno-scandic' identity that had been growing for the previous century. In the words of one activist: 'Swedes we are not; Russians we do not want to become. Let us therefore be Finns.' A petition circulated, but met with no worthwhile response. The artist Akseli Gallen-Kallela designed a black 'stamp of mourning' bearing a golden Finnish lion, which Finns duly glued to all their envelopes as a quiet protest about the Russian stamps. This is where we came in, with Eetu Isto's painting *The Attack* – the Maid of Finland, hanging on for dear life to her book of laws, while the double-headed eagle attempts to tear it from her grasp. The Maid of Finland is not scared, but shows a demeanour of grim resolve. A lantern of 'sacrifice' lies broken on the ground, its flame still sputtering with the fires of resistance. On the horizon, there is a faint glimmer of dawn, in spite of the stormy skies.

When it was first completed, the picture still did not have a name. It was hung in a house in Kaivopuisto, Helsinki, and shown only to an audience of invited revolutionaries. 'The observers,' wrote Eino Parmanen in his *Book of the Struggles*, 'stood amazed and in deep affection, many even with tears in their eyes.' Isto solicited suggestions for the title in the visitors' book, where also-rans included *Fantasy*, *Allegory*, and *Battle*, before *The Attack* was suggested by a friend's wife.

Would-be revolutionaries with an eye on the picture's propaganda value were already determined to make copies. It was photographed, and the negatives were used to etch copper plates for heliogravure printing. But the police had already uncovered rumours of an anti-Russian art exhibition somewhere in the city, and Isto was forced to flee his Kaivopuisto hideaway, grabbing the two-metre-high portrait and escaping through the window of the house, running for the docks and safety in Sweden.

Copies of the painting were soon in production, trickling into Finland from printers in both Stockholm and Berlin, including 10,000 smuggled into the country in heavy boxes marked 'anatomical preparations'. A policeman actually stopped one crate on the dockside at Turku, demanding to know what could be in such a large and heavy box. He was assured by some nearby students that it contained geological samples. Several other shipments came in along the Finnish smugglers' coast, where the thousands of islands and inlets afforded local fishermen with multiple opportunities to dodge Russian customs vessels and police inspections. *The Attack* also spread among American Finns in postcard format, and somehow made it into Russia itself by 1903, when unknown sympathisers were said to be distributing a version the size of a postage stamp for secretive supporters to cherish in their pockets.

When the day came for the new Finnish conscripts to enrol for their Russian army duty, more than half failed to show up. Bobrikov was granted dictatorial powers, but Finns were not pressed to join up, as the Tsar's army no longer trusted them anyway. This sudden frosty attitude towards the Finns caused new troubles for the Russians, when someone in the maritime office realised that almost all the pilots on the ships that arrived in St Petersburg were from the now allegedly disloyal Grand Duchy. One carefully timed strike among the pilots, and St Petersburg could be shut down from the sea. Hastily, the Russians convened a new pilot school to rush through some presumably more loyal men.

In 1904, Tsar Nicholas II went to war at the far eastern end of his new Trans-Siberian Railway, fighting a disastrous conflict against Japan. The Russo-Japanese War of 1904–5 has sometimes been called World War Zero for its use as a testing ground for many of the innovations of the later conflict – including the early designs for dreadnoughts, barbed wire, trench warfare, wireless telegraphy, and sea mines. But even as the Russian war machine was grinding into action, Finland risked becoming a fifth column of unrest on the Tsar's doorstep. Several anarchist groups hatched plans to assassinate Bobrikov, although all were beaten to it by a man supposedly acting alone. Eugen Schauman, a senator's son and former clerk who knew his way around the Senate building, sneaked in through a back door in June 1904 and accosted Bobrikov on the stairs.

Schauman had been practising with his Browning pistol for weeks, and was a sure shot. He fired off three swift rounds, all of which hit the governor-general. Then he turned his pistol on himself and shot himself twice in the heart, dead before he hit the ground. Bobrikov's many medals deflected two of the bullets, but the third shattered on his belt buckle and wrecked his stomach. He did not die until the following day, after a tense vigil in which the Russians were never quite sure what the Finnish crowd outside the hospital was praying for.

Condemned as a terrorist, Eugen Schauman was buried in an unmarked grave, although he was later moved to his family tomb in Porvoo. The site of the assassination is marked by a discreet plaque in the hallway of what is now the Finnish prime minister's office, reading in Latin:

Pro Patria Se Dedit ('For his country himself he gave'). As with Lalli of legend (see Chapter 1), Finland defined itself through brutal opposition to foreign influences.

There was some controversy over whether or not Schauman was really acting alone. Certainly, the Russians were suspicious that a prominent Swedish newspaper should not only report on the incident the following day, but have a photograph of the assassin ready to run, as if parties in Stockholm already knew it was going to happen.

It was also not lost on the Tsar's enemies that the Finns were ready for direct action, leading the Japanese secret service to plot a daring act of espionage, designed to distract the Tsar from the Far East by creating trouble on his doorstep.

The Japanese military attaché in Stockholm, Motojiro Akashi, was given a million yen in cash, and told to do everything he could to stir up the Finns. Akashi, a lone man 'worth ten divisions' in the eyes of the Japanese high command, hatched a plan to undermine Russia by starting a revolution in its Grand Duchy. He assembled an unlikely multinational group of agents, led by Konni Zilliacus, a committed revolutionary who acquired an aging tramp steamer, the *John Grafton*, bought in the name of a Stepney wine merchant and stocked with thousands of rifles, pistols, and rounds of ammunition, all bought by agents claiming to represent the King of Siam.

Owing to a misunderstanding with the aforementioned wine merchant, the *John Grafton* was also loaded with several hundred gallons of wine, which the Finnish crew had already begun to work through by the time the ship was in the North Sea. Zilliacus unwisely chose this highly stressful secret mission, with his crew unconvincingly disguised as members of the Southampton Yacht Club, to try to give up smoking – leading to an embarrassing set-to with the police in Copenhagen where he was caught trying to break into a tobacconist.

After several more misadventures in the Baltic, the *John Grafton* eventually reached the Finnish coast, which it located by unceremoniously ramming into it. Trapped in the shallows of Ostrobothnia, the crew began unloading their cargo, only to be surprised by a vessel from the Russian navy. Realising that time was tight, they ran up the red flag, saluted it, and then ran for dear life while a lit fuse sparked the onboard explosives.

The explosion of the *John Grafton* was heard two counties away. The Tsar's men inspected its twisted wreckage and fearfully reported on the likelihood that many hundreds of rifles that had been landed before the explosion. Although the revolutionary mission had been a failure, the mere fact of the existence of the *John Grafton*, and the possibility that it was only one of many ships, was a source of great concern to the Russian state. However, it had taken care of most of Akashi's money, and he would soon be run out of Europe after some of his meddling correspondence was made public; he ended up as governor of Taiwan. Konni Zilliacus fled to England, where he would write his memoirs and a cookbook. In one of those odd footnotes of history, his namesake son became the Labour MP for Manchester Gorton.

Revolution: Whites vs Reds

Despite such dangers in Finnish waters, with Russia's defeat and destabilisation in the war with Japan, Finland still seemed like a safer place for the Tsar than his own empire. Tsar Nicholas II came nowhere near Finland for the first decade of his reign, but became a regular sight there in the 1900s, after his security detail informed him that they could no longer guarantee his safety in Russia proper. Not seeing this for the awful portent that it was, Nicholas took to cruising the Gulf of Finland on his beloved yacht *Standart*.

'For the tsar, it is the only way to spend a real holiday,' wrote Baroness Sophie Buxhoeveden in her memoirs. 'While in Finland, he gave up formalities of the court and lived a more simple life. He got daily reports from his ministers in the capital, but they would take up only a part of his day. The greatest part he spent as he pleased, hunting, canoeing, or playing tennis, all of which are pleasing pastimes for the emperor.'

Finland was a pleasanter realm for Nicholas II partly because the defeat in 1905 had led to a general relaxation of his earlier Russification policies. With the Tsar conceding a 'Duma' (parliament) in St Petersburg after post-war protests, the Finns also gained a greater degree of political freedom, with the first decade of the twentieth century seeing the formation of several parties whose influence continues today – both the National Coalition and the Social Democrats, two of the major parties in modern Finland, began in slightly different forms in the brief thaw post-1905. By 1907 the Tsar was flexing his muscles again, and the Finns found themselves pressured to 'Russify' once more.

In 1914, Germany declared war on Russia, plunging the Tsar and his dominions into a conflict in Europe, and causing mass lay-offs in the Finnish timber industry, which lost many of its European clients. Otherwise, the early days of the First World War caused something of an economic boom in Finland, with massive increases in demand for Finnish paper, dairy products, and food to supply the Russian army.

In 1917, Russia's fading fortunes in the war and unemployment in its cities combined to form the events of the 'March Revolution'. Finland responded in July 1917 by proclaiming itself independent from Russian rule, a bold and somewhat foolhardy move for a state without its own army. Instead, the peacekeeping lay in the hands of two rival local militia, the right-wing Whites and the left-wing Reds.

The division of Finland into Whites and Reds is arguably the greatest of its national tragedies, all the more so because many of them shared similar aims. Most wanted an independent Finland – ironically the pro-Tsarist Whites in Russia refused to consider an independent Finland, whereas the Bolshevik Reds under Lenin paid lip-service to the idea of one, which they hoped would volunteer to rejoin Russia as a Soviet republic. With the collapse of Russia's political government in the second (i.e. 'October') Revolution of 1917, Finland became a site of simmering tensions, infested with nests of Russian soldiers with uncertain allegiances, and roving bands of militia.

The south of the country, its urban centres including Turku, Viipuri, and Helsinki, was claimed for the Reds, although a number of White politicians smuggled themselves out of the capital and formed a rump government on the coast at Vaasa, ahead of the Red Terror that saw over 1,600 White sympathisers murdered. Vaasa hence became the centre of the White counter-attack. Local White militia neutralised Red enclaves and Russian outposts with whatever weapons came to hand, including the confiscated Grafton rifles, mothballed in storage for over a decade, and now finally put to a revolutionary use.

The leader of the White military forces was the fifty-year-old Carl Gustaf Mannerheim, a baron of the Finnish nobility who had served thirty years in the Russian army. Mannerheim had enjoyed a relatively undistinguished career, specialising in two areas of expertise that were overtaken by technology and politics. He had previously been a cavalry specialist in the era that saw the introduction of the internal combustion engine. He had then specialised in Far Eastern matters, in the expectation that Russia would one day fight a rematch against Japan in Chinese territory – a war long on the cards, but forever postponed by the Russian Revolution. By 1917, he was a lieutenant general, the highest-ranking Finn in Russian service, and despondent at the treatment his country had received

Fleeing revolutionary Russia by the skin of his teeth, he arrived back in Finland to find himself appointed as the leader of the White forces, in command of an army of well-intentioned farmers, aging former officers of the disbanded Finnish army (idle for a decade), or soldiers, like him, whose service to the Tsar made others suspicious of their motives. Mannerheim led the White forces from their Vaasa redoubt in a campaign that would seize the important hubs of the railway network, pushing back against the Red forces and driving them ever further to the south and east.

His most controversial victory was at the Battle of Tampere in 1918, a hard-fought conflict over the city that straddled the railway connection to Helsinki. Tampere proved to be the decisive battle of what had become the Finnish Civil War – its fall would leave the Reds in the south open to attacks from either flank.

But Tampere was controversial because of the high loss of life. A series of men lost to Red snipers led to the indiscriminate use of grenades against any movement in buildings – sometimes with tragic results. A thousand Whites perished in the fight over the city, and double the number of Reds. But some ten thousand Reds were taken prisoner, many of whom died in custody of maltreatment, starvation, or disease. Mannerheim had accorded his opponents the military distinction of regarding them as enemy combatants – by his decree all surrendered Reds should be treated as prisoners of war, and accorded due process. But the flipside of Mannerheim's distinction, not immediately recognised by many of his supporters, was that Reds who broke the terms of their surrender would also be treated with military procedure. The implications of this only became clear in the aftermath of the White victory, when any attempts by Reds in occupied territory to stir up unrest, such as blowing up a bridge or assaulting a soldier, would be met with summary execution for acts of military espionage.

Mannerheim's own sister, who had worked as a nurse in Red Helsinki, had written to him pleading for merciful treatment for prisoners, arguing that the Reds she had met were good-hearted people with a sense of loyalty to an independent Finland. But her words were lost in a bitter conflict that set neighbour against neighbour, split families forever, and saw the settling of many petty scores under the guise of patriotism. The story of the civil war is rich with tales of petty fights and intimidations – the White soldiers in Lahti who stole the Reds' artillery when they left it outside a pub; the Red sympathisers in Jyväskylä who nailed shut all the doors of pro-White shopkeepers; the two Red prisoners in Viipuri shot for merely suggesting that they might be rescued by a counter-attack from over the border; the many lynchings and assaults conducted against men in Red areas seen as 'landlords', or women in White areas seen as 'Russian brides' (female Red supporters in trousers were often assumed to be combatants and treated as such; those in skirts merely as collaborators).

The resentment of the Civil War would simmer among the Finns for over a decade, and manifest in many petty acts such as the decision by the Finnish army in 1925 to build a pigsty over the site of Red war graves on the island of Santahamina. Such conflicts festered until the Second World War presented them with a greater enemy against whom they could unite. But even today it occasionally bubbles to the surface, in small, angry acts such as the vandalism of Mannerheim's Tampere statue.

The Jaegers and the King of Finland

There is another side to the Finnish Civil War, of huge importance at the time although it, too, has been swamped by later historical events, and that is the involvement of the Germans.

Mannerheim only accepted the position as leader of the White forces on the understanding that he would be leading Finnish soldiers. Ever the strategist, he was worried about the implications of winning the battle for Finland with foreign aid – there were already Swedish peacekeepers landed on the Åland Islands, whom he suspected of plotting to wrest the territory away from Finland. He was thus immensely angry and, eventually, grudgingly grateful for the arrival of troops from yet another foreign power, the Kaiser's Germany.

During the period of attempted Russification, many patriotic Finns, particularly from wealthier families with foreign connections, sneaked out of the country or were exiled for anti-Russian sentiment, and made their way through Sweden to Germany, where they enlisted in the German army. The 27th Prussian Jaeger Battalion, which fought for Germany in 1916, contained some 1,100 Finns. Eventually some 2,000 strong, they returned to Finland in the middle of the Civil War, bringing much-needed skills and experience to the White side.

The Jaegers arrived as an incredible morale boost to the Finns, although much to their annoyance, many of them were dragged out of their units to train less able men who lacked their experience. Just to whip up everybody's martial ire, the composer Sibelius cranked out a stirring hymn, the 'Jaeger March', to lyrics written by Jaeger Heikki Nurmio:

Deep is our blow, our wrath invincible,

we have no mercy, no homeland.
Our fortune rests on the tip of our swords,
our hearts cannot fail.
Our war cry rings, enchanting the nation
that is severing its chains.

And so on, only slightly ruined for modern ears by the chance echoes in its opening bars of the theme from *The Muppet Show*.

The Jaegers also brought some friends with them – 10,000 German soldiers of the Baltic Sea Division under the command of Rüdiger von der Goltz, whose arrival constituted a second front against the Reds. Mannerheim, who had spent the early part of the First World War fighting against the Germans as a Russian officer, was deeply mistrustful of the Kaiser's motives, rightly suspecting that Germany was hoping to secure influence over a new Finnish satellite state to keep it supplied with raw materials. He did have to concede that the Germans were vital in securing several southern sites, including Turku and Helsinki itself, where the arrival of German allies may have even saved Finnish lives by preventing a retaliatory bloodbath of Reds by victorious Whites.

Although the Jaegers are famous in Finnish history, and would form not only the core of the new army of independent Finland, but a powerful faction within the early Finnish government and institutions, the Baltic Sea Division is less well known. The Germans did not march in Mannerheim's victory parade in Helsinki, allowing Mannerheim and the media coverage of the day to remember it as a 'Finnish' achievement. According to von der Goltz's memoirs, published in 1920, this was his own idea in order to preserve the Finnish sense of achievement; he crept away with his men to fight on in Latvia, leaving the Finns to establish their newly won state.

Von der Goltz remained respectful and enamoured of Finland, commenting in his memoirs that Finland was the only place where Germans were still welcome 'with open arms'.

> Germany won a new friend, the only friend to remain true to it, who did not turn away ... with revulsion and disdain ... We Germans will not forget that about Finland. All of us, though, who were allowed to contribute to this ... are proud to have taken part in the sole surviving success from this world war.

It was not the last time that Finns found themselves alone, only to be rescued by German allies. This was certainly a contributing factor in the next request for aid from Germany, when a monarchist faction within the new Finnish government asked if the Germans could lend them a king.

The previous monarch of Finland, at least technically, had been Tsar Nicholas II, already dead by Bolshevik firing squad in Ekaterinburg. There were already factions within the government calling for a presidential republic, but monarchists, favouring a Swedish-style king, enjoyed a marginal majority at the critical time of May 1918. So it was that a Finnish envoy was sent scurrying to Kaiser Wilhelm

II, with a request that his fifth son accept a notional crown of Finland, and become its first king.

The son in question was unavailable, as was Duke Adolf Friedrich of Mecklenburg-Schwerin, who had been proposed as the grand ruler of a unified Baltic Duchy, incorporating not only Finland, but also Estonia and Latvia.

By September 1918, the Finnish Diet had its man, Prince Friedrich Karl of Hesse, the Kaiser's fifty-year-old brother-in-law. Rüdiger von der Goltz approved, noting that the prince and his wife were famously down-to-earth, and that it was this 'great straightforwardness and naturalness that recommended him to the democratically minded Finns.'

Although the parliament was still locked in debate, with the appointment of 'King Karl I' still not quite gaining the two-third majority required by protocol, the prince was confident enough to begin Finnish lessons with his wife. He embarked at a leisurely ninety minutes a day, which, in the author's own experience, would have allowed him to order a beer in a restaurant after only another year of study.

Truth be told, most Finns were less enthused about the aging Friedrich than they were about his dashing young son Wolfgang, already being billed as Finland's crown prince, and lined up for a meeting with eligible young Finnish debutantes in the search for a local bride.

But 1918 was precisely the wrong time to get into bed with Germany. Finnish hopes of securing German political support were fast dwindling, as was Germany's ability to keep its own house in order. It was Mannerheim who sternly warned the monarchists that Finland could not afford to be seen to ally itself with the defeated Kaiser's Germany, but as late as October 1918, there were still elements within the Finnish government trying to entice Prince Friedrich over.

In the end, it was Friedrich himself who called a close to the idea, asking for two months to consider the offer. By the time his self-imposed deadline had passed, Germany had been defeated, the Kaiser had abdicated, and the Finnish senate had instead approached one of their own, offering Mannerheim the role of Regent of Finland. Mannerheim returned from meetings in London with the news that the British would recognise the newly formed state of Finland on several conditions, including the cancellation of any invitation to any German monarch.

Friedrich ended the charade on 14 December 1918, officially rejecting the crown, and leaving Finland no other realistic option but that of a republic. Regent Mannerheim arrived back in his homeland two days later, and served in that role for six months, until elections returned the lawyer KJ Ståhlberg as Finland's first president.

But there is far more to this footnote of Finnish history than meets the eye. Although on paper it sounds like little more than an exchange of telegrams and some faffing around a possible political appointment, the plan to create a Finnish king was far more involved. At the time Prince Frederick Charles walked away from the idea, Finnish designers were already hard at work on his monograms and his crest, as well as the uniforms of his honour guard, hand-picked from the ranks of the German-trained Jaegers who had fought in the Finnish civil war. The carpets and fixtures for his palace (the former Imperial Palace, now the Presidential Palace) had already been ordered, and artisans from the Stockmann department store in Helsinki were already delivering his sofa.

His cool Deco couch and chairs were a matter of some controversy – delivered for a kingdom that would not exist, no official of the new republic would pay for them, and Stockmann was obliged to put on a special sale of almost-royal furniture. Some of these items miraculously survived, and would go on show in 2018 in a centenary exhibition of Finland's almost-king in Tampere.

The Kingdom of Finland was nothing but a fantasy. Its crown, designed but never made, was eventually created in replica in the 1980s by curious Finnish artisans. Its putative king died in 1940, as the Head of the House of Hesse. Two weeks after his funeral, an envoy arrived from the Finnish embassy in Berlin, and discreetly laid a wreath on his tomb. Crown Prince Wolfgang died in 1989, the last surviving great-grandchild of Queen Victoria.

Karelian Fever

Post-revolutionary Finland saw a robust and enduring entrenchment from the winning side, the victorious Whites. It was not a welcoming place for those who had supported the Reds, although occasionally there are tales of cheeky commemoration, such as the massive stone memorial to the Reds which suddenly materialised in a Turku graveyard in the 1920s. It had been dragged there overnight by stone masons, who sneaked it in by knocking down the wall and then rebuilding it before anyone noticed.

If the story of Finland's Reds seems under-represented in today's public life, it is because many of those that weren't killed in the conflict faded into the landscape of Soviet Karelia, or emigrated to North America or Australia. Although the split into Red and White is a common subject in many Finnish films and novels, few of these have been translated. The national memory of the revolution and/or civil war is one of White victory, and the sense that Finland, of all the Tsar's domains, was the only one to stay clear of Communism after the October Revolution.

Unwelcome in their own country, many of the socialist Finns chose to emigrate, swelling the ranks once more of Finnish-Americans in Michigan and Minnesota, and turning their enclaves abroad into strong outposts of left-leaning culture. In many cases they became miners in Michigan's 'Copper Country', embracing the name 'Red Finns', which actually derived from the dust on the miners' faces. Others willingly took over landholdings that previous owners had given up on, proclaiming the land too poor to properly farm.

Before long, the Red Finns ran into troubles in their new home, particularly as America itself began to turn against socialism and socialists. Their problem was compounded by a persistent rumour among Americans that Finns did not count as true Europeans, but were instead *Asian* interlopers, and hence should not be permitted to immigrate at all. Finnish writers had done themselves no favours in this regard by publishing numerous pamphlets and histories that proudly identified Finnish origins as being from somewhere east of Europe, such as the slightly dotty Georg Wettenhof-Asp, who published as Wettenhovi-Aspa, and who claimed in his *Suomen Kultainen Kirja* ('Book of

Finnish Glory', 1915) that Finnish had been the original language of mankind, and that they were the ultimate founders of all the world's great past civilisations. Other writers would claim that the Finns were a lost tribe of Israel, or even descended from the Japanese Ainu.

Such nonsense might sound frivolous in hindsight, but it formed part of a dangerous miasma of racism and innuendo, suggesting that Finns should be excluded from American society much as American society was already busily excluding the Chinese and the Japanese. Matters had earlier come to a head in a landmark court case in 1908, when a Minnesota public prosecutor attempted to block the immigration of seventeen Finns on the grounds that they were 'Mongol', and hence 'coloured', and thereby subject to exclusion under Minnesota's 1882 immigration law. Judge William A. Cant, forever remembered as a friend of the Finns thereafter, ruled that of all the new arrivals in the Americas, 'none were as fair-skinned as the Finns' – in its way, just as racist and unproven an assumption as the initial suit, but one that the Finns were happy to accept. Nevertheless, comments that Finns were 'Mongolian' in origin remained a matter of occasional notice in the American and Finnish-American press until the 1930s.

Not every Red Finn in America chose to stay, or even to return to their homeland. Many thousands volunteered to 'return' not to Finland proper, but to the newly established Soviet Socialist Republic of Karelia, a land that had never been politically part of Finland, but nevertheless enjoyed strong linguistic ties – Karelian being variously regarded as either a language cognate with Finnish or a mere dialect of it, depending on whom one asked. The volunteers answered the call from the Soviet Union for experienced loggers, farmers, and workers, who could be expected to help revitalise a deprived and backward economy. At the time, the leaders of Soviet Karelia were two exiled Finnish communists, Edvard Gylling and Kustaa Rovio, determined to create the paradise denied to them in Finland proper, and to set an example for the rest of the Soviet Union to follow.

Finns, and in some cases their Finnish-American children brought along for the adventure, would constitute less than 1% of the Karelian population, which was primarily Russian, but with 40% Karelians – Finnish-*speaking*, but not Finns per se. For many, the venture was undertaken as a utopian quest, as recalled by the former settler Mayme Sevander, who wrote in her memoirs of a breathless ode by a forgotten poet, celebrating the Finns' sacrifice:

Far away to Asian expanses
Our comrades are leaving again
Knowing so well they stand no chances
Of winning without taking pains.

Karelia was not actually *in* Asia – it was still on the western side of the Ural Mountains – but the use of the term reflects the degree to which emigrants considered themselves to be travelling far, far away. Recruitment offices in New York and Toronto targeted ethnic Finns. They came to Karelia's aid by arriving not only in person, but with far more efficient tools – one Russian study observed that a Canadian lumberjack, armed with a frame saw, was four times as efficient as his Russian counterparts. Skilled Finnish migrants formed a large part of the labour force at the Petrozavodsk Ski Factory, and by the 1930s were also put to work making furniture, with the vague hope of a new export market to bring in foreign currency. Others were put to work at the far end of the production chain, to run farms that would not only help reduce the Soviet Union's reliance on food imports, but also provide feed for animals.

The dream of a Finnish Karelia was drastically damaged by political changes in the Soviet Union, as the rise to power of Josef Stalin created an environment hostile to ethnic difference or 'bourgeois' lifestyles – the Finns' life was anything but comfortable, but they still enjoyed substantial privileges above those of the local population. Samira Saramo's book, *Building That Bright Future* assembles multiple first-person accounts from Finns in Soviet Karelia, turning progressively sourer as the years wore on, and the Finns were at first resented, and then hounded by the local Russians. In 1937, a new Soviet directive ordered that they no longer speak Finnish, but were obliged to use Russian – a command that was even expected to apply to teachers at Finnish only schools. Once invited as foreign guests, the Finns were now shunned as unwelcome, 'anti-Soviet' nationalists.

Shortly afterwards, in the Stalinist Great Purge, thousands of them were murdered – at least 268 Finnish-Americans were uncovered in one mass grave site alone. Modern-day excavations of multiple grave sites have found bodies bound and shot in the back of the head, along with smashed vodka bottles given to impart courage to weary executioners, and discarded cans of meat, thought to have been a grim reward for poverty-stricken firing squads.

The Finns, of course, were barely of statistical relevance in a terror that consumed the lives of a million people, in which the former Soviet obsession with 'class enemies' transformed instead to a more all-encompassing search for 'enemies of the people'. Gylling and Rovio, the former leaders of Soviet Karelia, were among the victims, summoned back to Moscow and executed in 1938. The events led to a deadpan Finnish joke in poor taste, that Stalin was a great man because he killed a lot of Communists.

Some did survive. The Finnish-American opera-singer Katri Lammi, once a star at the Petrozavodsk theatre, was bundled onto the back of a truck to be taken off to the prison camp at Lime Island. A quilt wrapped around her shoulders, she sang out defiantly from the back of the vehicle:

Wide is my Motherland,
Of her many forests, fields, and rivers!
I know of no other such country
Where a man can breathe so freely.

The song was a calculated jab at her captors, the 'Song of the Motherland' from the film *Circus* (1936), about an American refugee who comes to Russia and falls in love with the ideals of the Soviet Union.

Years later, Lammi returned from prison, a broken widow, aged before her time. She died in an old people's home on Valaam island, a forgotten remnant of a different kind of Finnishness, built up and then destroyed by the Soviet Union.

Racing the Storm

Back in Finland, the debate on what 'Finnishness' should be only intensified after the foundation of an independent state. Many of those who fought to establish it found themselves marginalised and unwelcome in the new nation, including Gustaf Mannerheim himself, heroic general of the Whites in the Civil War, who stood unsuccessfully for president and then slunk away into quiet semi-retirement, muttering dire portents about the need for more military funding and the threat of a Russian attack.

Communism had been declared illegal in Finland in 1918, further pushing sympathisers into the arms of the Soviet Karelians, but that didn't stop various front organisations and left-wing parties gaining large shares of the vote – the remaining Red Finns remained a voting bloc with some strength, threatening to turn Finland into a Soviet state by force of democratic will. Women, meanwhile, who had had the vote in Finland since 1906, were a major influence on the ratification of a 1919 Prohibition law (the *Kieltolaki*), which turned Finland into an officially alcohol-free state (complete with 'fortified' teas and speakeasies) for the next thirteen years.

With a strong ethnic-Finnish voting bloc to pander to in the American Midwest, US food aid helped stave off starvation in the war-wrecked country, leading to the 1920s Finnish slang term for sponging: 'living off [President] Hoover'. Finland turned its attention to Europe, conducting barely 1% of its trade with the Soviet Russian state on its border. As Josef Stalin rose to power in the Soviet Union, Russian rhetoric about Finland became increasingly agitated, painting it as a far-right dictatorship, run by a junta of Red-hating rebels. By the 1930s, Stalin was secure enough in the Soviet Union to begin talking of regaining 'lost' territories from the Tsar's era.

Mannerheim referred in his memoirs to a sense of 'racing the storm' in the 1930s, as the League of Nations struggled to keep reins on disputes. One of the international body's only successes was its ruling that the Åland Islands, disputed between Sweden and Finland, should be Finnish territory, winning Mannerheim a diplomatic victory and keeping the islands in Finnish hands to this day. But elsewhere the League was increasingly powerless, leaving the Finns on their own as Stalin's negotiators arrived to demand concessions in the south-east. When Finland had been a Grand Duchy, the fact that its borders were so close to St Petersburg was not an issue. Now it was independent and anti-Red, it represented a dangerous threat practically on the city limits of what was now the city of Leningrad.

Russian behaviour became increasingly bullish, and the situation increasingly fraught, while Mannerheim, now back in the administration, demanded better funding for Finland's military to deal with a rising threat. Eventually, he resigned in frustration. Barely two days later, on 26 November 1939, Russian artillerymen on the border shelled one of their own positions, creating an immediate crisis, accusations of a Finnish attack, and a Soviet 'counter'-offensive. The Winter War had begun.

5

The Jaws of Peril: 1939–1944

Some of the Winter War trenches on the Raate Road are still maintained, kept clear of debris and vegetation, walled in with planks and wooden pilings. You can wander among the snaking front lines, crouched half-hunkered against imaginary shrapnel, and stare through the peaceful forests at the places where once the Russians were.

There are howitzers and armoured vehicles scattered outside the Raate Road Museum, and the baked ruin of a Russian tank, twisted and fired in some terrible conflagration. Inside the museum proper, the battle over the Raate Road is picked out in a vast diorama with toy vehicles and little painted figures and railway-model fir trees. It shows the moment that the elite Soviet 44th division mistakenly decided to enter Finland uninvited, via the Raate Road.

On 5 January 1940, amid temperatures that fell below forty degrees celsius, the Russians, unused to skis and not all that keen on snow, were ambushed by 300 Finns.

Even the model itself is scary. The gunmetal-grey Russian column of tanks and troop transports is scattered across thirty feet of model forest, strewn with model horses laying on their side, and toy soldiers trampled in the Hornby train-set snow. White-clad Finns, ghosts in the snow with pistols, knives, and axes are dotted through the model forest. It looks as if several toy buses have hit several herds of toy reindeer, the Manson family let loose on a Nativity scene. Roughly halfway down the column, there is figure in a white dress, face down in the snow with a pistol in her hand.

Outside the museum, in a vast area of cleared forest, there is a figure-of-eight pathway with a shamanistic-seeming structure at its centre. Seen from a distance, the Winter War Monument looks like four sets of giant antlers leaning on each other. Its graceful curves support a lattice-work of bells – 105 little chimes ringing in the wind, one for each day of the hostilities.

It sits in the middle of a blasted field with jagged rocks, numbering some 20,000 – one for every life lost on both sides. It is, supposedly, 'polynational', designed in 2003 by Erkki Pullinen to meet the needs of several museums and organisations on both sides of the border, to commemorate the lives of both sides. But the Finns around the monument tell a different story. My guide, Vesa, pats one of the large boulders reverently, explaining: 'These are the Finns.'

He leans down and scoops up a handful of gravel.

'This,' he whispers, 'is the Russians.'

There are also separate monuments on the road itself. The one for the Finns is fraught with all the pretensions of modern art. It is a big ... thing ... by the roadside. Some say it is Stalin's accusing finger. Others that it is a howitzer at rest. Nobody seems to know. Somewhere, an artist found a bit of metal, welded it to a plinth, and sold it to the Finnish government.

The Russians have their own monument, too, by the

road in the middle of the woods. It is a weeping woman, sunk to her knees in anguish, clutching at a cruciform staff for support. Past the statue is an area of boggy ground, crossed by walking on duckboards across the sodden earth. Somewhere beneath your feet are the unrecovered bodies of seventy-nine Russians, who never made it out of the marsh.

The Winter War

Despite only occupying six years of Finland's history, the Second World War was definitive in establishing the Finnish sense of nationhood and state of mind. Its repercussions echo today, in Finnish men's continued obligation to perform national military service, in candle-lit autumn graveyards, and stoically observed flag days.

For the Finns who lived through it, it was greeted as the end of the Red–White rivalry, with Mannerheim (dragged out of retirement again) calling on the people to put aside their old enmities to fight a greater foe. It briefly cherished the unlikely dream of a Greater Finland stretching all the way to the White Sea, before rudely awakening the Finns with the loss of 10% of their territory. The Maid of Finland suffered the loss of one arm (the Petsamo region, reassigned from Russia in the 1860s, now snatched back for its nickel mine) and some serious liposuction around her hips (most of Karelia) – some 410,000 Karelian Finns fled west to be settled in post-war Finland.

The war also solidified the Finns' reputation for bloody-minded tenacity: they were admired in the international press for their resistance against overwhelming odds; then pitied for their abandonment to the whims of realpolitik with the Russian switch in sides; then reviled for signing a controversial co-belligerency pact with the Nazis. The Finnish term *sisu*, for sheer guts, briefly entered the international lexicon; indeed, many Finns are still surprised when visiting foreigners have never heard of it, since it was a worldwide trending term in the 1940s.

The Russians had begun by demanding territory from the Finns for strategic purposes – the Hanko peninsula, former sight of Princess Alvild's legendary Viking raids, as a port for the modern navy, and territory in the south-west to roll back the border from Leningrad. When these 'negotiations' bore little fruit – the Finns being unwilling to simply hand over territory because Stalin wanted it – his foreign minister Vyacheslav Molotov ominously declared that it was 'time for the soldiers' to do the talking.

Sixty-five men, women, and children died in the first bombing raids on Helsinki, while Molotov snidely commented that the Soviet aircraft were only dropping 'food parcels' for the local population. In later battles in the east, Finnish soldiers would return the culinary insult by hurling 'Molotov cocktails' at the Russians – the first use of what is now an international slang term for a petrol bomb.

In the eastern Finnish town of Terijoki, the Finnish Communist Otto Kuusinen suddenly declared the foundation of the Finnish Democratic Republic. Terijoki had only recently been evacuated by the Finns, which makes one wonder where Kuusinen got his population from, but the move was plainly calculated to reignite the Red/White stand-off, offering Finnish Reds an apparent alternative to the incumbent government. At a strategic level, it was designed to allow the Soviets to fight a war in Finland without declaring one, since they could justify an invasion of Finnish territory as 'coming to the aid' of a government facing rebel unrest, redefining the *actual* elected government of Finland as insurgents. Kuusinen's puppet state was overwhelmed by current events – the prolonged Finnish resistance to Russia would prove to be so powerful that even Stalin would eventually negotiate with the real government, cancelling any potential value of the Red splinter state. Very briefly, the Democratic Republic of Finland was assigned a huge parcel of land in Soviet Karelia, in return for ceding more strategically valuable land near St Petersburg. Mannerheim would later attempt to push a Finnish advance into those 'new' lands, only to face resistance from some of his own men, who objected to invading territory that was only part of Finland because their enemies said so.

Today, Terijoki (or Zelenogorsk, as it is now known) is still a station on the train line from Helsinki to St Petersburg, but the mainline trains don't even slow down for it. Blink and you'll miss it, a bit like the Finnish Democratic Republic. Kuusinen's proclamation was also very obviously an act of Russian propaganda, to the extent that it actually disgusted many of Finland's honest-hearted Reds, and led them to proclaim their allegiance to Mannerheim. One story of the Winter War recalls a former Red serving in the Finnish army, blithely observing that he was pleased that the 'Butcher in Chief' who annihilated them at Tampere was now in charge of defending the whole country.

Mannerheim ran his defence out of a train-based command centre and a scattered series of buildings in

Mikkeli. The real action was down on the Karelian Isthmus where Finland met the outlying regions of Leningrad Oblast, and where a 'Mannerheim Line' of fortifications significantly slowed the Soviet advance.

The Soviet numbers were overwhelming, but the soldiers were poorly trained and badly supplied. Many of them had yet to work out that it was inadvisable to throw a grenade ahead of oneself when skiing; many lacked adequate winter clothing; few had any experience of winter fighting. The Finns literally ran rings around them, luring them onto lake ice and dynamiting it under their tanks; attacking tactical bottlenecks of moving columns, leaving thousands of troops stuck behind damaged vehicles; ambushing them from the trees. The Finnish reputation for *sisu* gained some of its most notorious examples. Regardless of the size of an attacking air squadron, the Finns would always send at least one plane up against them, hoping for a lucky shot against over-confident bombers. There are stories from the Winter War of Finns with pistols single-handedly trying to take out tanks by aiming through the tiny eye slits; of attacks targeting not the Soviets' heavy gear, but their morale-maintaining soup kitchens; and of night attacks where Finns fell upon Russians huddled two to a sleeping bag in cold conditions, and slitting just one throat per pair, leaving the other to wake up next to a cold and bloody corpse.

Low-tech was the order of the day. Finland's most famous sniper, Simo Häyhä, notched up 505 kills in the Winter War, using a basic rifle without a scope. He claimed it allowed him to keep his head a fraction lower, and avoided the glint of the scope's glass potentially alerting his targets.

Such behaviours all served to fatally bog down the Soviet advance. The Soviet plan on the Raate road in the north was to cut Finland in half at Oulu. Instead, despite outnumbering the Finns five to one, the attempted blitzkrieg rush to the coast advanced with agonising slowness. Often, when the Russians did advance, it was only because the Finns had hatched another devious ambush a mile ahead.

Häyhä served in the Battle of Kollaa, in which the absence of roads pushed the Finns onto skis and the Russians into artillery bombardments. Kollaa has become another of the iconic moments in the history of Finnish *sisu*, notable particularly for the emphasis in its traditions on the surly tension between Finnish commanders and the men on the ground. When Major-General Woldemar Hägglund asked his subordinate Aarne Juutilainen if Kollaa would hold, he got a very Finnish response.

'Kollaa will hold, unless we are *ordered* to run away.'

Not even Mannerheim believed the figures. He sent a brusque communiqué to one of his front-line commanders, demanding fair and accurate assessments of military actions, and not wild claims such as that of killing a thousand Russians in a single night. An officer at Taipale responded with characteristic Finnish bluntness, telling his commander-in-chief that he had a pile of a thousand Russian rifles, and Mannerheim was welcome to come down and count them himself.

Winston Churchill flagged the success of Finland in its fight against Communism in his 'House of Many Mansions' speech, 20 January 1940.

Only Finland – superb, nay, sublime in the jaws of peril – Finland shows what free men can do. The service rendered by Finland to mankind is magnificent ... Many illusions about Soviet Russia have been dispelled in these few fierce weeks of fighting in the Arctic Circle. Everyone can see how Communism rots the soul of a nation; how it makes it abject and hungry in peace, and proves it base and abominable in war ... If the light of freedom which still burns so brightly in the frozen North should be finally quenched, it might well herald a return to the Dark Ages, when every vestige of human progress during two thousand years would be engulfed.

Finland fought on alone. In March 1940, the combatants came back to the table to negotiate, resulting in the Peace of Moscow that ceded parts of eastern Finland to the Soviets. The desperate Finnish holding action had served its purpose, keeping the country from falling to the Soviet Union at a terrible cost. The treaty specified that the roads, bridges, and towns of Karelia should be left intact, but when the Russians moved in, they discovered they had forgotten to stipulate that the Finns should remain. They marched into ghost towns, devoid of people, and often with the cultural treasures stripped away. In churches all over Finland, a signed decree from Mannerheim can usually still be found framed on the wall, awarding a medal to the 'mothers of Finland' for their own sacrifices.

The Continuation War

The end of the Winter War came as something of a surprise for the Finns in Helsinki, who had heard nothing but stirring tales of heroism, and had started to assume that the strong resistance could go on indefinitely. Mannerheim had a far better idea of the exhaustion of his men and resources, and knew that the time was right to call it before his hard-won line began to buckle. Having served in the Russian military for thirty years, Mannerheim was well aware of his former masters' policy of seizing as much territory as possible, with no intention of holding it, and then ransoming it back to the enemy for gains elsewhere.

The peace lasted for two whole months before the Russians began pushing for more concessions. Mannerheim had warned all along that this would happen, and had spent many weeks pleading with the government that the war was not over, merely on hiatus.

In 1940, the poet and professor Veikko Koskenniemi wrote lyrics to 'Finlandia', a musical piece by Sibelius that dated back to 1900 and the height of the Tsar's Russification programme. It remains one of the songs that is most likely to rouse the passions of the Finns, possibly even more than their national anthem – its opening, at first sight at least, seems rooted in the struggle for Finland's independence in the nineteenth century, only for allusions to gather of the conflict that was still raw in Finns' hearts.

O, Finland, behold, your day is dawning,
The threat of night has been banished away,
And the lark of morning in the brightness sings,

As though the very firmament would ring.
The powers of the night are vanquished by the morning
    light,
Your day is dawning, O land of birth.
O, rise, Finland, raise up high
Your head, wreathed with great memories.
O, rise, Finland, you showed to the world
That you drove away the slavery,
And that you did not bend under oppression,
Your day has come, O land of birth.

I have cornered Finns at parties and restaurants, and asked
them open-endedly to tell me what this song means to
them, curious as to whether they associate it with the 1900
tune or the 1940 lyrics. Universally, Finns have recalled
sights of snow and combat. Universally, they have begun
humming the tune and mouthing the lyrics. Universally,
their voices have cracked on the penultimate line *'ja ettet
taipunut Sa sorron alle'* ('And that you did not bend under
oppression').

It became something of an anthem of the Finns' sudden
counterstrike against the Russians, which began in June
1941. It is remembered in Finland as *Jatkosota* ('the Continuation War'), in Russia as the opening salvo of the Great
Patriotic War, and in Germany as Operation Barbarossa.
In a controversial move, Finland signed a 'co-belligerency
pact' with Hitler's Germany, resupplying its own forces
with crucial German materials, but also allowing German
troops to transit Finland in secret, ready to fall upon the
Soviet border in a surprise attack. Mannerheim remained

wary of the Germans, as he had been in 1918, and was keen to stress that he had not formed an alliance with the Germans, merely agreed that since both had a common enemy, they would fight alongside one another. This distinction was lost on many Finns, particularly in the north of the country, where the German divisions were welcomed as inheritors of the old Jaeger goodwill of the Civil War days, and received with such open arms that Finns were heard to grimly jape: 'The Russians took our men, and the Germans took our women.'

In imitation of the Jaegers of old, a number of Finnish men had also volunteered to serve in the German army, forming a component of the 5th SS Panzer Division. Comprised of foreigners from the Baltic region, from which it drew its historically minded nickname *Wiiking* ('Viking'), the 5th SS Panzer Division fought on the Eastern front, at Stalingrad and in the Caucasus, at Kharkov and Kursk, before the increasingly defensive actions saw them moved back into Poland and Czechoslovakia. By then, the several hundred Finnish volunteers had long been withdrawn and sent back to Finland to bolster the troops in the Continuation War – they had been ordered home at Mannerheim's request, and he forbade any further enlistment of Finns in German battalions.

Moscow fought back over the airwaves, with hectoring broadcasts by the Continuation War's very own Tokyo Rose, Aino Kallio, nicknamed 'Moscow Tiltu' – a girl's name associated in Finnish popular song with that of an overly credulous teenager. She shared the propaganda offensive with Armas Äikiä, who had been the Minister of

Agriculture in Kuusinen's short-lived Democratic Republic, and who now harangued Finns over the radio about
the fact they were effectively bolstering Hitler's regime. So,
too, did Greta Kivinen, or 'London Jenny', a well-spoken
announcer for the BBC's Finnish-language short-wave pro-
gramming, who repeatedly pleaded with Finnish listeners
to see the error of their ways.

Nine thousand Soviet prisoners of war were drafted as
slave labourers to make up for the lack in the region's man-
power, in order to help the Germans create the infrastructure that they required to fight in the manner to which they
had become accustomed. Conditions in the nearly 200
camps scattered around Finland ranged from 'tolerable' to
'inhuman', but as Oula Seitsonen argues in his *Archaeologies of Hitler's Arctic War*, the shadow of this unmentioned
labour can still be seen in modern times: 'many of the
modern roads in Lapland trail the ... Second World War
tracks, and the cadastral plans of several northern towns
follow those of the German barrack villages.'

There was, Seitsonen suggests, also a 'punishment camp'
for Jewish prisoners of war somewhere in Finland, although
his research has yet to officially locate it, It was, presumably
nowhere near Syjärvi, where in one of the most absurdly
unlikely incidents of the Second World War, Finnish Jews
serving in the army set up the only field synagogue on Nazi
front-lines, and held services in front of their SS comrades.
Even so, the Jews fighting alongside the Nazis did so amid
recurring rumours that when the war was over, 'the ship
would be waiting' to take them away to an unknown fate.
One of them, the Jewish field doctor Leo Skurnik, was even

awarded the Iron Cross after fearlessly carrying wounded SS men out of harm's way during an attack. He then bluntly refused to accept it, with the immortal words: 'I wipe my arse with the Iron Cross.'

Offended by this, the Nazi authorities demanded that he be handed over, only for his commanding officer to refuse to give up his best doctor. Two other Finnish Jews also refused a German medal, although not quite so colourfully. Having encountered Jewish soldiers on a trip to inspect the Nazi lines, Heinrich Himmler buttonholed the Finnish prime minister, asking him what he was going to do about the Jewish question.

'We have no Jewish question,' was the fantastically Finnish response. He was, however, economical with the truth – the former head of the state political police, Arno Anthoni, would face trial after the war for handing over eight Jews, including a baby born in Finland, to the Nazis under the guise of a broader 'deportation of undesirables'.

Meanwhile, Lapland was in thrall to a series of terror attacks, as roaming platoons of Soviet partisans sought to tie up the troops in the most heartlessly economical way possible, by targeting random civilian settlements. Most of these partisan atrocities went carefully unreported in the Finnish media – to have given them publicity would have given the Russians what they wanted.

Despite such retaliations, the Continuation War was an unprecedented strategic success. Finns, aided by strong German advances at their flanks, snatched back the lands that had been lost in the Winter War and kept on going. Helsinki presses and publishers, newly pro-German, fulminated about the need for *Finnlands lebensraum* in the East. The attitude informed one of the most entertainingly braggart propaganda songs of the era, 'To the Urals' (*Uraliin*), the tune of which had formerly been used in a recording by the Finnish-American singer Katri Lammi. Her original version was an exotic fantasy about Cossack riders and the romance of the mountains and steppes:

> Maiden of the Urals,
> Dark, and beautiful, with eyes of blue
> I should warm her icy chest with kisses
> The guide is about to get a kiss from the girl
> It banishes the pain from his chest.
> On the steppes, even at night,
> The Ural maiden rests sheltered.

And so on. The new version, however, managed to troll most of the Allies, while summing up Finland's self-identification as a lone champion of justice, expressing the unlikely hope that the Russian retreat would take the enemy past the mountain range that marked the geographical edge of Europe. From her lonely Soviet prison cell, Lammi would surely have approved.

> To the Urals, and beyond
> We hear the Russian boots as they scramble
> 'Why did I trust England?'
> Sighs Stalin as he tears out his hair
> 'Why didn't Finland listen to Tiltu and Äikiä,
> Even though everything they said was soap and rattling?'

To the Urals, to the Urals
Now even Finland is on the way.

Someone help the Ivans
The scary Finns are getting all up in their Cabbage-land
But it doesn't seem to help
Even if the Yanks are commiserating
'Coz the Japs are striking westwards just as quickly as
      they can
And the Germans are blowing Allied [shipping]
      tonnage up into the air
To the Urals, that's the job
The Russians run like there's fire under their boots.

Mannerheim's men took back East Karelia all the way to
the shores of Lake Ladoga, snatching not only Finnish land
but also chunks of Soviet Karelia, only to stop tantalisingly
short of Leningrad. There was substantial argument in
Finland about the wisdom of this action – regaining stolen
ground was one thing, but actively invading and appro-
priating Russian territory was not necessarily what many
Finns had signed up for. Such issues also characterised the
affable, ever polite but increasingly apprehensive commu-
niqués between Mannerheim and Churchill, as the British
Prime Minister gingerly warned the Finnish Marshal that if
matters continued in this way, Britain would be forced to
declare war on Finland, despite their long friendship.

'I wish I could convince Your Excellency that we are
going to beat the Nazis,' wrote Churchill, 'It would be most
painful to the many friends of your country in England

if Finland found herself in the dock with the guilty and defeated Nazis.' Britain did eventually declare war on Finland, at least on paper. But it was perhaps with Churchill's warning in mind that the Finns executed the next and final turnabout of their Second World War. As a Soviet counter-offensive pushed the Finns out of Karelia and drove them back to their 1940 borders, the Finns turned on their German allies, ordering them out of the country, and then attacking any who were slow to get the message.

The Lapland War

This 'Lapland War', named for the northern Finnish realm where most of the Germans were stationed, led to the destruction of most buildings north of the Arctic Circle, as both the Finns and Germans demolished any sites that might be used by their enemies. The Germans, in particular, got the blame for this, to the extent that it is still something of an aggressive tradition in Finnish Lapland of shaking matchboxes at German tourists.

The Germans were certainly taken aback by the sudden reversal – one can still sometimes spot the faded traces of graffiti in the area reading: '*Danke für nichts*'. They left behind wives, girlfriends, and children, although many hundreds of Finnish women chose to leave with their German husbands, the subject of Virpi Suutari's 2010 documentary *Auf Wiedersehen Finnland*.

The Germans fled towards the safety of the Norwegian border, leaving behind a hellscape of smouldering buildings, a rain of burning papers falling from the sky, and a land strewn with mines. For years to come there was a risk of exploding reindeer – hundreds of local people also lost their lives to landmines after the war, and some 2,000 were injured, a fact only really publicised in 2012. A year later, arguably explaining why it had been kept quiet for so long, a metal detectorist looking for Nazi memorabilia in Kemi was killed by a grenade he had found.

But the Lapland War, while a cruel and devious reversal, would serve Finland well after VE Day. Although some Finnish politicians would be locked away for their dealings with the Nazis, Finland itself avoided occupation or invasion. Although the Second World War would cost Finland some 10% of its territory, it remained free, albeit in hock to the Soviet Union for war reparations – despite the many thousands of miles of borders shared by the Soviet Union with other countries, only Finland and Norway among them were democracies with market economies. Appointed by the Finnish parliament as an interim ruler, Gustaf Mannerheim ended his active career as President Mannerheim, serving until March 1946, when the transfer to peacetime was considered done.

In the decades since, there have been many subtle shifts and redactions of local history that shield and obscure the wartime era. Sometimes, they are in plain sight, like the Alppimaja ('Alpine Lodge') district on Oulu's Tirolintie ('Tyrol Street'), named for the Austrian *jägers* once quartered there. Others are less well-known. The patriotically named Kalevalankartano ('Estate of the Kalevala') in Oulu, for example, was originally built as the SS Officers' Club, and come to think of it, does look rather Teutonic. It also turns out that the world-famous Santa Claus Village, in Rovaniemi, is built on the site of a former Luftwaffe airbase, and that the year-on-year expansion of the Village threatens to wipe out many archaeological materials from its previous existence.

In a school in Vuotso, outside Sodankylä, there is a standard 1939–44 *Isanmaa Puolesta* ('For the Fatherland') memorial, which features a death in 1959 – a local boy, killed by an unexploded bomb. Such tragedies are included by the Finns in official accounts of the 'war dead', for a war that is still not over until the last of its materials cease to kill.

6

In the Cold: 1944–1995

The city is known in Russian as Kostomuksha – the Finns insist on calling it Kostamus. It is only thirty miles on the Russian side of the border, but the road is closed, shutting down much of the town's trade. It is home to the strictly controlled Kostomuksha nature reserve, as well as a local iron-ore refinery.

There is a statue in the Friendship Garden outside the town's Culture and Sports Centre. It depicts two men sitting on a pair of tree stumps, mid-discussion. One is Alexei Kosygin (1904–80), who for the last sixteen years of his life was the Premier (prime minister) of the Soviet Union. With body language that inadvertently echoes that of Tsar Alexander II's statue in central Helsinki, he is offering something, but here it is a sheaf of papers topped by a map of the local area. He is in mid-discussion with his friend, Urho Kekkonen (1900–86), who for the last three decades of his life was first the prime minister, and then the president of Finland. Kosygin's legs are nonchalantly crossed. Kekkonen sits upright, leaning his forearms on his thighs, listening with active attention.

Unveiled in 2013, the statue celebrates the lifelong friendship of the two statesmen who steered Russo-Finnish relations through the mid- to late-twentieth century. They are depicted discussing the deal that would revitalise the economies of both Finland and Soviet Karelia, a massive 1970s construction scheme that would put thousands of Finns to work in Russia, building not only the Kostomuksha ore refinery, but much of the town that served it. Urho Kekkonen remains something of a local hero in Soviet Karelia, a stoic friend of Russia and the Russians, who kept the two countries from coming to blows during the years of the Cold War. Until cross-border tourism was shut down by the 2022 conflict in Ukraine, Finnish coach parties would arrive in Kostomuksha to see the smoke sauna where Kosygin and Kekkonen hammered out their deal, and the log cabin where earnest signage proclaimed that 'Kekkonen slept here.' They would hear stories about the Finnish politician who was awarded the Lenin Peace Prize in 1980 (yes, apparently there is a Lenin Peace Prize), and whose efforts helped revitalise the economy of what was now *Russia's* backward Karelia region.

Kekkonen remains a recognisable figure throughout the former Soviet Union, including Tallinn, where Finns fresh off the ferry from Helsinki used to be confronted by the image of his face, his iconic black spectacles resprayed an attention-grabbing pink, gurning out at them from the terrace of the Kekkonen pub. Kekkonen, in fact, had been instrumental in the project to build Tallinn's Hotel Viru in 1969, which was contracted to a Finnish construction company, and described in later times as a cultural 'Trojan horse' during the Cold War, with its own KGB listening post to spy on the guests. It became an early tourist destination for Finns, who found little to buy in Tallinn's Soviet-era shops, and so instead spent their marks on booze, food, and *activities*. Hotel Viru became a site of varied international relations, where Soviet dignitaries would sneak in to watch the LA Olympics (which they were supposed to be boycotting) on Finnish television, and where prostitutes on the staircase would demurely flash the soles of their shoes, on which their prices had been written.

It is also, one suspects, no coincidence that in 1956, when Finnish-Americans in Minnesota concocted an invented tradition to trump St Patrick's Day among the Irish, they came up with 'St Urho', a fictional Christian missionary who had, supposedly, banished all the grasshoppers from medieval Finland, thereby saving the nation's similarly non-existent grape harvest. The fake saint, who is celebrated with prolonged drinking a convenient twenty-four hours before the equally boozy feast day of St Patrick, derived his name from Kekkonen, who became president of Finland in the same year, and remained in office for the next thirty.

Back in his native Finland, Kekkonen has a more contested legacy, regarded by his enemies as a power-mad would-be dictator, ever ready to play the Russia card when his domestic standing was threatened, clinging to his authority for decades, even as old age rendered him increasingly frail. His supporters, on the other hand, still regard him as a superhuman statesman, the only person in Finland willing to take up the poison chalice of running the country during its long years in the shadow of the Soviet Union. Friends and enemies alike cite the television recording of the presidential voting in 1978, in which a Finnish announcer read out the electoral college results in groups of five to an expressionless audience of politicians, dispassionately and monotonously, without any of them acknowledging the absurdity and unanimity of the decision: 'Kekkonen, Kekkonen, Kekkonen, Kekkonen, Kekkonen.'

It was a dirty job, but someone had to do it.

Stella Polaris & the Weapons Caches

The war left enduring traces in Finnish infrastructure. In Lapland, the new roads built to aid military access now afforded deeper penetration into lands that had once been occupied solely by Saami, hastening the displacement of Finland's indigenous people. To the south, there was a flurry of new building to accommodate the 410,000 refugee Karelians who now needed to be settled in friendly territory. In many cases, this involved a fast-track adoption of pre-fabricated houses, mass-produced to a general design, known as a *tyypitalo* ('typical house') or a *rintamamiestalo* ('frontline-man house'). The concept had existed for over a decade, but was now implemented nationwide, and can still be seen today, in occasional districts of identikit 1.5-storey houses, the bedrooms tucked under the roof in such a way as to be impossible for a tall Finn to stand up in. Sociologists have observed that this, too, exerted an invisible pressure on later demographics – a *rintamamiestalo* is a snug dwelling for a modern-style nuclear family with two kids, but would not support a larger or multi-generational extended family.

The Karelians also brought with them a religious crisis, since they represented more than two-thirds of all the Orthodox believers in Finland, their home churches now cut off. As a result, Finland passed an emergency law authorising the construction of new Orthodox churches around the country – an ironic reversal of the days of early Swedish rule in Karelia, where the building of new Orthodox churches has been forbidden.

In the closing days of the war, some elements of the Finnish armed forces began making plans for a prolonged insurgency. With no guarantee of how treaty negotiations or post-war reparations would proceed, two Finnish colonels commenced a bold and controversial plan. Aladár Paasonen and Reino Hallamaa supervised the evacuation of cratefuls of Finnish intelligence documents across the Baltic Sea to Sweden, along with several hundred intelligence personnel, in what would be known as Operation Stella Polaris ('Northern Star').

Later in 1945, many of the officers sneaked back across the border into Finland, although several of them remained in Sweden as 'Swedish' intelligence officers. Paasonen oversaw the conversion of thousands of intelligence documents into microfilm, much of which was then sold to several intelligence agencies among the Allies, including to *Seta Samuli* ('Uncle Sam'). Much of the original material was subsequently burned at a Swedish rubbish dump, and the degree to which the Finnish government had or had not colluded in the ransacking, destruction, and sale of state secrets would remain a touchy subject in the years that followed.

With a watchful eye on Russian occupations in eastern Europe, two other Finnish colonels, Valo Nihtilä and Usko Haahti, embarked upon a scheme to secrete firearms and ammunition around the country, all the better to have a ready-made rebellion up their sleeves in the event of a Russian occupation. Their original plans, to have enough supplies in hand to outfit 8,000 men around Finland to fight as guerrillas, found such strong support that an estimated 35,000 could have been equipped with the weapons that were eventually hidden away.

When the Russian occupation failed to materialise, the weapons caches turned into a festering and dangerous secret, ever at risk of being discovered and upsetting the delicate post-war balance of power. The veteran Lauri Kumpulainen was caught selling ammunition on the black market in Oulu – ammunition that he had liberated from a local weapons cache. Fearful of reprisals from his fellow soldiers, whose attitude had already taken on certain elements of a secret society, he confessed to the Allied Control Commission that was overseeing the armistice out of its offices in Helsinki's Hotel Törni. The ACC passed the case on to the Finnish security police, as the investigation snowballed from what at first had seemed to be a simple case of under-the-counter wheeler-dealing, to the uncovering of concealed weapons for seditious purposes, to a nationwide conspiracy.

Moreover, it was a matter of politics whether the plotters in the 'Weapons Cache Case' amounted to stout-hearted patriots or would-be terrorists. Finnish cinemas had only recently been showing films like *The February Manifesto* (1939) and *The Activists* (1939), both of which had glorified the cunning and bravery required to forge a Finnish republic out of an earnest resistance to Russian oppression. Now, both films were banned in order to avoid offending tender

Soviet sensibilities, and Finland was under strong pressure to punish Finns who were behaving exactly like the heroes who had founded the republic in the first place. In an additional legal issue, there was no actual law on the Finnish statute books that the conspirators could be said to have been breaking.

This was remedied with a shameful compromise in 1947 – a law after the fact under which the Finns could then be retroactively tried, in order to justify over a thousand arrests and convictions. The true size of the Weapons Cache Case – the *Asekätkentä* in Finnish – is liable never to be known, as many of the caches were discreetly returned to military bases before they could be discovered. With a command structure that went right up to the highest ranks, there were so many arrests that popular slang rechristened Helsinki's Sörnaianen Prison as 'the General Staff'. Held, often for months without trial, for breaking a law that had not existed at the time they were accused of breaking it, many Finnish veterans became under-dog heroes. In one case that grimly outlined the resolve and bravery of the officers involved, the decorated aerial ace Urho Lehtovaara, a Knight of the Mannerheim Cross, overpowered his interrogator, seized the man's pistol, and shot himself in order to keep the secrets safe.

Some have claimed that the Weapons Cache Case was precisely the sort of seditious behaviour that might be used by the Soviets to *justify* an annexation of Finland. Others, including the conspiracy's historian Matti Lukkari, have argued quite the opposite – that like the *John Grafton* incident forty years earlier (see Chapter 4), the very fact of the conspiracy's existence served as a deadly notification to the Russians of the size and scope of a likely Finnish resistance. In spite of multiple prison sentences dished out to the alleged offenders, few careers seemed to have been damaged by the revelations. Indeed, many of the conspirators, much to the Soviets' annoyance, went on to be promoted to high ranks, such that by 1966, the entire top echelon of the Finnish military comprised officers who had not only been implicated in the conspiracy, but served time for it.

Finlandisation

During the era of the Cold War, Finland walked a tense line, carefully preserving a neutral status while sharing a 1000-kilometre eastern border with its greatest historical enemy. Finland's seventh president, Juho Paasikivi, had formerly been the ambassador to Moscow, and navigated the country through treacherous waters. Finland may have preserved its independence in the Second World War, but it remained perilously close to the Soviet Union and Soviet influence. 'Wisdom,' said Paasikivi with a shrug, 'begins with acknowledgement of the facts.' And the fact was that should conflict ever break out again, Finland would once again be likely to face the Soviet Union alone.

The Paasikivi Doctrine was one of 'active neutrality', with Finland doing its level best to not make any sudden moves that might annoy the Russians. This was continued by his successor Urho Kekkonen, in office from 1956, under whom Finland exercised careful censorship of inflammatory or anti-Soviet media, and affected a cool disinterest in NATO, in order to avoid being press-ganged into the Warsaw Pact.

Some undiplomatic diplomats, carping from the safety of the free world, began to refer to 'Finlandisation', with the implication that Finland had been somehow infiltrated and tainted by the Soviet Union. During the long reign of President Kekkonen, the term *Kekkoslovakia* was also used as a pejorative by the Finns themselves, suggesting that Finland was practically in the Soviet Union's pocket. But Finland's delicate position cut both ways. Finnish politicians were just as fearful of NATO, since if war broke out and the Western powers mounted an attack on Russia through Finnish airspace, the Finns would be unable to stop them, and would then face the risk of a Russian counter-strike similarly crossing Finnish territory.

In 1961, Kekkonen summarised his political position to the United Nations by saying that the Finns wanted to be 'physicians rather than judges' in superpower politics. 'It is not for us to pass judgement nor to condemn, it is rather to diagnose and to try to cure.' To some extent, he was even successful – Finland's war reparations to the Soviet Union, intended to cripple it post-war, were not only paid in full, but in such a manner as to turn Finland into one of the Soviet Union's major trading partners. As conditions thawed, Finland was reframed not as a former enemy suffering financial punishment, but as an example of the kind of peaceful trade relations it was possible for the Soviet Union to have with the outside world.

Contemporary Finns are insulted by the notion that their country is in 'Eastern Europe'. They try at all times to push the notion that they are one of the 'Nordic Countries', practically Scandinavian in their outlook and background.

But the mid- to late-twentieth century saw Finland pursue its careful neutrality in the shadow of Moscow, with restrictions on criticising the Soviet Union only finally relaxing in the late 1980s, as the rise of Mikhail Gorbachev heralded the downfall of Communism. Ironically, this would also cause a deep recession in Finland, when many of the country's east-facing trade contacts collapsed – the Finnish GDP fell by 10%, double the damage done to it in the Great Depression of the 1930s. However, by the 1990s, with the Soviet Union's power dwindling, Finland could finally come in from the cold. In 1992, with the Soviet Union finally gone, the Finnish Defence Minister Elisabeth Rehn even raised the possibility in a speech that the weapons cache conspirators of old had performed a valuable patriotic duty, and deserved a pardon.

From Eurovision to Europe

Meanwhile, with wartime associations inadvisable, the sense of Finnishness retreated once more into myth, albeit myth that was carefully sanitised for an international audience. Throughout the years, Finland's Eurovision Song Contest entries represented the usual carnival of nutters, offering ill-considered ditties about nuclear war, meaningless lyrics about waterfowl, and even an awful attempt at reggae. In the midst of it all, in 1977, Monica Aspelund delivered a beautiful, moving song about doomed love beneath the Aurora Borealis – 'Lapponia', translated into six languages, charting high in several countries' hit parades, and usually mistranslated as some sort of tourist brochure. This is the dreadful English version:

If you need to get away
I know someplace where we can stay
Far away from the city, it's peaceful every day
Why don't we get on a plane tonight
And head for the Northern Lights
Where you can be happy
So sing along with me now.

Despite being initially commissioned as an advertising jingle to sell Lapponia-brand sheds, the original Finnish lyrics are very different: a fantastic and chilling evocation of ancient Lapland, laden with menace and wonder. Here it is translated from the original Finnish:

That girl is a witch
Who conjures with destinies
Without company or solace
And so she weaves her magic
Creating with the power of spells
So with sorcery she may summon a man.

Said man duly arrives, a 'human man of Earth' in the lyrics of the original song, who falls in love with her, only for her to fly away, *Käy tulella taivaan ja loitsut kaikuen soi* ('She goes with the fire of the sky and the spells echo'). Aspelund's lyrics are rich with the cadences of the *Kalevala* and the archaisms of Saami sorcery, but go and listen on YouTube: it will sound nothing like what you first imagine.

It's difficult to think of something quite so heavy-metal as this topic, but Aspelund's lyrics were shoe-horned into a piano melody by Aarno Raninen – it would be thirty-three years before the rock band Northern Kings gave it the properly bombastic version it really warranted. But the fate of 'Lapponia' only goes to show the immense pressures on Finnish creatives to somehow cram their rich poetic traditions into the demands, or supposed demands, of the international mainstream. In a country with less than 5.5 million people, it perhaps only makes sound business sense to sing in English and tick the right boxes for MTV. Finns speak perfect English by necessity, and have little trouble integrating themselves into the Americanised hit parade in the forms popularised by bands such as Hanoi Rocks, HIM, and the 69 Eyes. But a few strike out, like the folk group Värttinä, determined to hang onto their Finnishness in subjects and language, drawing their lyrics from ancient spells and love ballads. Finnish artists, in many media, often face a brutal choice between remaining forever a big fish in a small pond, never filling a venue bigger than a town hall, or removing so much of their Finnishness to sing in English and appeal to the Americanised MTV world that they hardly seem to be Finns at all.

If there is anywhere that Finland in the late twentieth century achieved unexpected worldwide fame, it is in the technology sector, where the chance confluence of several forces and innovations made Finland a prime mover in the global digital economy in the 1990s. The Nokia Corporation began in the industrial revolutionary era of the nineteenth century that saw lumber mills and cotton mills springing up near the rapids of Tampere. It had slowly accreted from a rubber company, a wood company, and several other ventures, moving almost by accident into telegraphy and electricity generation in the twentieth century. By the 1980s, a lucrative contract with the Finnish armed forces had caused the company to experiment with wireless telephony, and the canny purchase of its leading competitor left it a market leader in the growing sector of what were first called 'car phones', and then, as they became smaller and more efficient, 'mobile phones'.

By 1987, Nokia had established a global standard in 'second generation' phones, which is to say, ones that could not only call other phones, but also send text messages. Within a decade, Nokia had become the world's largest manufacturer of mobile phones, and would remain so for thirteen prosperous years, until everybody and his dog had a cell phone, and competition from Android and iPhone operating systems crushed the company's lead.

For many foreigners born at the close of the twentieth century, Finland is a place associated not with any historical narrative, but with such modern developments in digital technology – not just the big-bang of mobile communications in the space of a single generation, but the rise of applications and open-source software. Linus Torvalds, a student at Helsinki University, released an operating system in 1991, which he would literally give away to the online community. Linux, as it came to be known, is now the basis of millions of computers and systems, and only the most fundamental and widespread of many Finnish initiatives in open-source software and content.

Finland was aided in this international market by a major political change in 1995, the hotly contested decision to enter the European Union, bolstered by a citizens' referendum that returned a lukewarm 56% vote in favour of it, somehow turning into a two-thirds majority in parliament when the politicians enacted on the information from the 'advisory' referendum. Finland's *yes* vote gave the nation access to millions of consumers across a free trade area, as well as the tantalising prospect of joining the single European currency, which it eventually did in 2002 at the end of a three-year transition period. To this day, Finns of a certain age have given the government the side-eye, convinced that the conversion rate of the old markka to the euro was a cunningly concealed sleight-of-hand designed to obscure nationwide price hikes.

The transformation went both ways – Finland might have been an insignificant land of trees and lakes, with a population so small that it could fit twice over into contemporary London, but its accession to the European Union also brought substantial geopolitical changes to the parent organisation. For the first time, Europe now had territory extending deep into the Arctic Circle, as well as a land border with Russia. Nor was this all bad news for the Russians, whose special relationship with the Finns now gave them an effective backdoor to the European market. The budget airline Ryanair began what at first might have been regarded as a pointless service to Lappeenranta in eastern Finland, although the smart money soon realised that it amounted to stealth trips to the edge of Russian airspace, depositing passengers a mere three hours by bus from St Petersburg. Lappeenranta, in particular, became a new Russian riviera, like the gulf resorts of the Tsarist era, packed with EU goods for sale, a daytrip away from a metropolis with a population that matched that of Finland itself. The railway lines and trunk roads into Russia formed an active two-way trade, with Russian goods only having to make a single journey before entering a multinational consumer base in its millions, and foods from Finnish supermarkets, just about to hit their sell-by date, finding a new lease of life in the Russian re-sale market.

In October 1994, the *Los Angeles Times* ran a series of vox pops from the voters in the referendum, asking them how they felt about the massive transformation. Hannu Olkinoure, the editor of the newspaper *Kauppalehti*, rejected the notion that it was business that was the crucial factor.

'It's politics and security that's driving us,' he said. 'Something in me says there is a certain momentum, a chance for us to point out that we belong to the Western Hemisphere before Russia gets stronger.'

Brigit Lindström, a retired librarian, was one of the undecided voters who swung at the last moment in support of European membership.

'It's better for Finland,' she told the *LA Times*, 'because we won't be alone.'

7

The Landscape of Thorns: 1995–2022

Linnunlaulu ('birdsong') now comprises parkland around Töölö bay, an inlet of the Baltic that sits like a lake in the middle of Helsinki. A pathway snakes around the water's edge, hosting joggers, dog-walkers, and strollers. Just off the track, there is a 2.7-metre imposing stone slab, bearing a familiar symbol of three triangles within a circle, and a list of dozens of names.

It looks like any other war memorial that one might expect to see in a European park, although this is nothing to do with any war. It is the *Itsekkyyden Muistomerkki* ('the Monument to Selfishness'), erected by Greenpeace in 2010, bearing the names, districts, and party affiliations of 129 Finnish politicians who voted in favour of nuclear power.

It is an oddly mobile monument. Before it was fully carved, it sat outside the Finnish parliament building like a gravestone, bearing the ominous PR-nightmare legend on a sash: 'Do you want your name here?'

Since its completion, it has wandered the city like Banquo's stony ghost, popping up in slabby scorn outside the railway station, before finally coming to semi-permanent rest next to Töölö bay. One imagines certain politicians having the recurring nightmare that they might wake up to find it at the foot of their bed like the head of some Mafioso's prized racehorse.

The *Monument to Selfishness* is a fantastic icon of modern Finland. Its initiator, the marketing manager Veera Juvonen, has a masterful grasp of propaganda, and a suitably Finnish bluntness when it comes to naming and shaming the politicians. The permanent, enduring implications of nuclear power are carved in suitably long-lived stone, granite that will last for millennia, like the nuclear waste itself, long after the transient day-at-the-office that the voting surely comprised for many of its participants.

The *Monument to Selfishness* is the result of the controversy over the Olkiluoto power plant which can supply between 22–36% of all Finland's power requirements, depending on how many of its reactors are working. Defenders of Olkiluoto counter that it is an order of magnitude safer than Chernobyl, and has an environmental footprint substantially smaller than that of, say, the 120,000 windmills that would be required to replace it with green energy. It was also intended as the main pillar in fulfilling Finland's emission-reduction obligations under the Kyoto Accords – sometimes, one gets the impression, as ever, that the Finns are one of the only nations actually taking it seriously. In a quintessentially Finnish battle of wits and politesse, protestors outside the facility were beckoned in for a tour, to see its technology for themselves, but refused, perhaps understanding how accepting such an invitation might play into the hands of their rivals' public relations.

Some Finnish wags have even suggested that Olkiluoto itself serves as a monument to the spirit of the twenty-first century, not in terms of the hope of cleaner, safer nuclear power, but as a preposterous boondoggle that has run so far over budget that it is now 'too big to fail'. The construction of its third reactor, originally scheduled for completion in 2010, but not online until 2022, was dogged by safety considerations and code violations, as the strict parameters of nuclear power plant construction foxed the skills of an immigrant workforce. Having promised to absorb any cost overruns, the original construction company has backed out, leaving the project still unfinished. With projected final costs now standing at €8.5 billion, the lead companies on the project busied themselves in a finger-pointing battle over who should take responsibility for the many delays, while the media archly reported that Olkiluoto was now one of the most expensive structures in the world, with an estimated cost greater than that of Europe's Large Hadron Collider.

Meanwhile, digging continued at nearby Onkalo for the construction of a nuclear waste disposal vault suitable to keep radioactive materials undisturbed. Finns argued over the best way to post danger signs that will still be legible in 100,000 years' time. After discussions over monoliths and symbols, or a 'landscape of thorns' made from giant concrete spikes, the general consensus seems to be that the best policy is to hope that future civilisations simply forget it is there at all.

While construction continued to stall on the third reactor, the Finnish parliament voted for construction to begin on yet more generators, with more modest aims. It was this decision that led to the commissioning of the *Monument to Selfishness*, encapsulating not only the mistrust of many voters in the long-term safety of nuclear power, but in their elected representatives' apparent willingness to throw good money after bad.

Although energy issues hound politicians all over the world, Olkiluoto and Onkalo have some uniquely Finnish qualities. One gets the sense with Olkiluoto that many of its problems have been caused *because* of the Finns' traditional diligence in following rules and regulations. And Onkalo's impressive temple of radioactivity is only possible in Finland, where the rocks have already had several billion years untroubled by quakes and tectonic movements, and it seems to be worth risking storing nuclear waste within them for a few paltry thousands. At least Finland *has* a scheme for permanent disposal of nuclear waste.

Satan & Santa

Finland in the twenty-first century enjoys an international footprint far outweighing its meagre 5.5-million population. Its most conspicuous and, frankly, unexpected achievement came in 2006, when after decades of novelty acts, petrified jailbait, and weary lounge singers, Finland's entry to the Eurovision Song Contest swept the boards with a landslide victory. From the moment it won the pre-selection Song for Finland, 'Hard Rock Hallelujah' was clearly something of a lark. The rock band Lordi, attired in horror masks, with batwings and a battle-axe that shot fire, belted out heavy-metal bombast a world away from the kum-ba-yah internationalism of most Eurovision winners:

> The saints are crippled
> On this sinners' night

Lost are the lambs with no guiding light
The walls come down like thunder
The rock's about to roll
It's the arockalypse
Now bare your soul

Fortunately, most of the Catholic countries couldn't hear the lyrics properly. Even more luckily, Eurovision's recently inaugurated continent-wide tele-voting began around the time that half the Western world's pubs were evicting their giggling students and embittered goths, ensuring a 'protest vote' that propelled Lordi to unprecedented heights. The morning after the night before, the Finns suddenly found themselves not only part of the international community, but sitting at its very centre, having inadvertently won a contest with more viewers than the Oscars.

In London, the Finnish ambassador was hauled over the coals by the BBC, asked if he felt his country's culture was best represented by horned demons singing about Armageddon, and was too shocked to make the logical riposte that the British entry that year had featured a creepy rapper in a yellow leather jacket, standing in a classroom full of off-key schoolgirls.

The likelihood that many of Lordi's votes were bestowed ironically was lost on many Finns, who collapsed into exuberant triumphalism. For a nation that barely seemed to care what Eurovision was before May 2006, there was suddenly dancing in the duck ponds and excitable rooftop yells of 'Arockalypse!' The country went Lordi crazy, with the introduction of Lordi pizzas, Lordi calendars, Lordi masks, a Lordi comic, and a Lordi restaurant. Although much of the euphoria has now faded, the band's presence can still be felt in their hometown of Rovaniemi, where their demonic handprints adorn the local square. Musically, rock remains the drug of choice among many young Finns; the bored visitor can easily entertain themselves by timing how long it takes for Bryan Adams or Bon Jovi to turn up on the radio, and there is something rather sweet about the laundry section in Finnish supermarkets, which offers washing powder for whites, colours, and blacks for all the heavy-metal T-shirts. Famously, Finland has the most death metal bands per capita of any country in the world.

At the time of Lordi's success, Finland's other popular international claim to fame was in financial difficulty. Santa Park in Rovaniemi had been founded in 1998 by a UK-based corporation, funded by an intricate web of Finnish interests, including the airline Finnair, the Finnish post office, and a Finnish TV channel. For a country only recently integrated into the European Union, the prospect of a Santa-themed theme park was a wonderful piece of synergy, drawing on off-hand references in folklore to Father Christmas living in 'Lapland', and deviously rushing to put such a park in the Finnish part of Lapland, as opposed to, say, Norway's. Rovaniemi was an ideal location, sufficiently far from Helsinki to be reachable by a romantic overnight sleeper train, but also with air connections to the rest of Europe. Seasonal charter flights could transport large quantities of foreign tourists for a Christmas experience complete with real snow, real reindeer, and a convincingly avuncular Santa Claus. It was also far enough north to offer a reasonable chance of seeing the Aurora Borealis, and conveniently close to the physical line of the Arctic Circle – always a good photo opportunity. In 2009, the majority ownership of the park was transferred to two local Finns, who continue to push it as a global Christmas destination, including sleigh rides, a trip to Santa's workshop, and the ominous-sounding elf show.

My Homeland is Finland

Finland aspires to be a classless society. All men are equal when they are sitting in the sauna – a truism taken to literal conclusions in the Finnish army, where salutes are not required in addressing fellow nudists. Finns have little time for bespoke tailoring – regardless of one's profession, the unity of air-conditioned environments behind the triple-glazed windows, and the ubiquity of the snowstorms outside, soon favours a population in ski-wear in the street, and shirtsleeves in the office.

When summer rolls around, the Finns strip off with barely concealed glee, embracing the brief warmth in a flurry of lakeside barbecues and skinny-dipping. Sometimes, to the outside observer, they seem to take even the fun a little seriously. Ask a company director what he is doing at the weekend, and more often than not he will wax lyrical about his simple log cabin and the pleasures of chopping wood by a smoky fire. Particularly in the north, outside the metropolitan areas of the south, most Finns are only a couple of generations removed from farmers and foresters. Government healthy-eating initiatives have gently pressured them to take more salad and eat less lard, the calorific demands of pushing around a computer mouse somewhat dwarfed by the previous dietary requirements of woodsmen and milkmaids. Modern Finns remain wary of obesity and alcoholism, both easy temptations in an era of American super-sized portions and all-you-can-eat buffets.

Finland's education system is the envy of the world, prompting frenzied conferences as far away as Shanghai to attempt to work out the secret of Finnish kids' success at school, despite spending the least amount of combined time on classes and homework of any industrialised country. Speaking from first-hand experience, a lot of the success of the Finnish education system is down to the simple fact that it is chock full of Finns, gently cherished by a social security system that ensures square meals for all and a good home environment. The Finnish education system is also, to all intents and purposes, free of charge. Given a choice between idling one's way through a master's degree or entering the workplace to pay tax, many Finns simply take the student option, packing Finnish industry with graduates.

The tension in Finland comes in the second generation, where parents recently arrived in the middle class often have trouble persuading their offspring to put in the school hours required to stay there. Finland is not crime free – certain suburbs, in particular, have statistically unremarkable incidents of robbery, burglary, and drugs – but the problem that vexes many police to a greater extent is juvenile delinquency, not of hopeless thugs from broken homes, but of over-entitled rich kids who have grown up thinking that everything should be handed to them on a plate, and troubled by the realisation that work is still required.

Finnish education also happily calves off the more practically minded into vocational training in their teens, creating a ready army of cooks, beauticians, hairdressers, plumbers, carpenters, and electricians. In one of many beautifully simple and palpably beneficial incentives in Finnish law, all households are eligible for an annual tax break for home improvement and domestic services, as long as the money is spent on accredited labour. This generates massive demand for painters, decorators, builders, child-minders, and cleaners, finding ample employment for many vocational school graduates, but also ensuring that their work is run through the system and taxed. Not only is Finland mercifully short on cowboy builders, but homes are suitably ready to brave the next harsh winter.

Finland spent much of the late twentieth century attempting to worm its way into the international community. It joined the European Union and embraced the euro with great alacrity. It lucked into the worldwide exponential growth of mobile telephony, and scored several software hits, including the ongoing spread of Linux, and the unstoppable fad of *Angry Birds*, and *Clash of Clans*, the latter being the most popular online game in the world from 2012 to 2014, and still today the most popular download worldwide in Apple's app store. Affluent Finnish yuppies are the quintessential snowbirds, thronging to the Canary Islands, Crete, and Thailand in the winter months, to clog beaches, bars, and diving schools. But internationalism does not seem to be quite as welcome at home. Finland takes its quota of refugees, but immigrants have a tough time fitting in with such a complex and peculiar language, and into a population that is already naturally wary of outsiders.

The canny foreign observer can racially profile the genetic background of the average Finnish crowd with some degree of success, into elfin, flaxen-haired Swedes, impish, dark-haired Finns, almond-eyed, high-cheekboned Saami, and the occasional pointy-nosed Russian. But Finnishness, that national trait so nobly fought for, was defined for decades as a genetic and ethnic phenomenon. To be Finnish, one had to be from Finland; one had to have great-aunts from Karelia and a shed in the forest, an ancestor who once worked on the tar boats and a grandfather with a funny story about the Winter War. Finnishness, ever since the semi-legendary Lalli, has been about standing one's ground against new-fangled foreign ideas and arrivals – an idea that has returned to bite the nation's think-tanks in the cosmopolitan twenty-first century, when European citizens can up stakes and move to Finland with only the merest scribble of paperwork, when tourists from (whisper it ...) Russia can make or break the takings of a summer spa resort, or when the best chance of securing jobs at the local mill is attracting the interests of Chinese venture capitalists.

The average Somali or Thai has substantially greater difficulty integrating into such a privileged sense of Finnishness, particularly when faced by the usual right-wing spite common to urban areas, and an epicurean deficiency peculiar to Finland, that is strongly resistant to any 'foreign' food that is not pizza or a kebab. Nor might one really expect them to – for every gruff and unemployable Finn on the dole, snarling into his beer that some immigrant has taken his notional job, there is a Somali in a puffa-jacket and a bobble hat, skulking with his friends outside the railway station and bemoaning the pointlessness of having to learn Finnish when his ultimate aim is to drive a taxi in South London.

In the TV series *Mogadishu Avenue* (2006), the writer Jari Tervo made a bold and uplifting statement of unity by simply having the multi-ethnic cast sing the theme song – a rainbow coalition of races all belting out *Kotimaani Ompi Suomi* ('My Homeland is Finland'). His point, common to multiculturalists the world over, was that these people were born in Finland, went to Finnish schools, grew up speaking Finnish, and now were paying Finnish tax. Was that somehow not enough? But there was also a melancholy irony in his choice of song. In a country where the local deaf sign for 'blue' still requires the speaker to point at their own eye, and where 'pink' is denoted by a stroke of one's own cheek, the lyrics of the song allude to nativist assumptions only partly dispelled by merely being born in Finland.

> There was I born
> And thence my thoughts return from the countries of
>   the world
> Land of my father, language of my mother
> How much I love thee.

Getting into Finland as an immigrant is by no means an easy ride, not the least because making the grade does indeed entitle the applicant to a jackpot of social welfare, free education, and residence in the 'happiest country in the world'. There is no citizenship exam, per se, as there is in many other countries, but access is only granted after meeting stringent linguistic criteria. Having neglected, like an idiot, to realise I could have spent the previous fifteen years learning the far easier and just-as-qualifying Swedish, I became one of the poor souls assembled in a library exam room for the five-hour Finnish language test, the final hurdle to becoming a true Finn, with a small 't'. Amid strict anti-corruption measures, our photo-IDs checked every sixty minutes to make sure there were no ringers taking the test on others' behalf, my fellow entrants and I were subjected to a quiz steeped in Finnish identity politics.

It was not merely a matter of the language itself with its consonantal gradation, vowel harmony, internal declensions, and fifteen noun cases – it was the topics under discussion: what *kind* of sauna is out of bounds at the health centre? Did the police catch a family illegally fishing, or illegally picking mushrooms? What were the merits of green energy? Was the woman vegan, or was it her dog? *What* made the neighbours complain about the smell of foreign food? For the ultimate test, I was obliged to perform two monologues that would have taken any Finn far beyond the limits of their everyday comfort zone: to calm down a woman weeping in an elevator, and to haggle for a discount at an electronics store.

I was Finnish enough by that point to be scandalised at the notion of not wanting to pay sticker price – such negotiations seem all-too southern European to the Nordic mind. But thrift was becoming a new buzzword among the Finns, particularly in straitened times caused by huge economic downturns. The most visible damage was done by the sinking of the Nokia Corporation, which went from being a world-beating powerhouse to a far smaller, leaner tech company. With phones its acknowledged 'core' business in the late twentieth century, Nokia divested itself of almost everything else, including the rubber company that lent its name to the slang term for wellington boots – a pair of *nokias*.

By 2011, when the company announced a 'strategic partnership' with Microsoft, the writing was on the wall. Despite enduring popular conceptions of Nokia phones as robust and long-lived, consumers were flocking to flashier operating systems like those of the iPhone and the Android phone. By 2014, Nokia's cellphone division had been merged entirely into Microsoft Phone, leading to a series of lay-offs and redundancies that eviscerated the local telecomms market. Nokia remains a player in a number of future technologies, and may well rise again to world-beating status, but for now it employs far fewer Finns than it did at its 2006 peak. Nor are there necessarily huge numbers of jobs at some of Finland's other big-name companies – *Angry Birds* continues to be a money-spinner for Rovio Entertainment, for example, but the company itself operates in four countries, and only has 480 employees. Global belt-tightening has affected Finland as much as anywhere else, and this, in turn, has led to frictions that threaten life in utopia.

The question of Finnishness in a wired world found its ultimate artistic expression in a truly bonkers enterprise, seen by both the right and left wings as a triumphal illustration of their concerns, when the national television broadcaster YLE funded Gilbert Lukalian's production of *The Marshal of Finland* (2012), a film about Mannerheim, made in Kenya with an all-black cast. Presumably, for some earnest commissioner in an air-conditioned Helsinki meeting room, this was a good idea, stretching precious euros by filming in a cheap location, generating massive publicity for a televisual event, and demonstrating to the world that the story of Mannerheim was so internationally alluring as to attract the interest of African filmmakers.

The Finns went into uproar. A poll in the tabloid newspaper *Iltalehti* unconvincingly argued that 90% of Finns would refuse to tune in. The right went into conniptions about the sight of the hallowed Mannerheim being played by a black actor, while even the liberals were heard wondering if the whole thing wasn't an elaborate double bluff – a facetious, knowing carnivalisation of Mannerheim's reputation by depicting him in a Z-grade movie. People wondered, and are still wondering, to what extent the Kenyans were piously telling a story (leading man Telley Savalas Otieno certainly seemed serious about his role), or cynically milking gormless media lefties for boondoggle funding.

It all went to show, in a world where you can buy a Mannerheim cookbook, a Mannerheim comic, and a Mannerheim puppet show, that the word Mannerheim is almost as sure-fire a money spinner with Finns as the word Moomin. YLE certainly generated vast publicity and newspaper column inches, getting not only their movie but also a six-part documentary about the making of the movie. And they had generated 'debate', in much the same way that children taunt each other with imaginary blinking powder. But their decision was also divisive and underhand, taunting the audience with a provocative gesture, and daring them to raise objections and sound like racists.

In 2013, an altercation at the Jyväskylä City Library led to several men hospitalised with knife-wounds. The affray had begun at a speaking event about 'the Finnish far right', which members of the far right had tried to disrupt. Although, truth be told, the majority of the defendants turned out to be either Swedish-Finns or actual Swedes – the country across the Baltic exporting some of its own political agitation to its former possession. In the 2010s, this took the form of the 'Finnish Resistance Movement' (*Suomen Vastarintaliike*), an offshoot of a pan-Nordic 'national front', pushing Hitlerism, anti-Semitism, and the acceleration of racial conflict through violent provocation. Banned in 2019, the organisation is rumoured to have rebranded in several other forms, not least as the 'spontaneous' torchlight procession that can annually be found wending its way through the streets of Helsinki on Independence Day, ending at the memorial to the Finnish *Wiiking* SS at Hietaniemi and, incongruously, at the grave of Gustaf Mannerheim, who would have given them short shrift if he were alive.

But in the ferment of Finnish political parties, the anti-immigration, anti-Europe Finns Party (formerly the *Perussuomalaiset*, translated as 'True Finns', or more literally, the 'Basic Finns') has made exponential gains, coming in second in the 2019 general election, with 17.48% of the national vote, leaving the Social Democrats a mere two tenths of a percent in the lead, feverishly wheeling and dealing among the smaller parties to cobble together a coalition that excluded them. The European press widely attributed the True Finns' increased popularity to a scandal the previous year in Oulu, in which several immigrant men, hailing from Tajikistan, Afghanistan, and Iraq were tried and convicted for sexual offences committed against underage and vulnerable Finnish girls, whom they had been grooming through social media.

A 'True' Finn canvassing in one election accosted me outside the supermarket in Muurame, and offered me a free sausage if I wanted to discuss all those immigrants who were taking over.

'I am one of them,' I replied.

This was not as awkward as the moment in business class on a flight from London, when a high-ranking executive in a well-known Finnish company, with whom I had previously been having a perfectly nice conversation, suddenly commented that he was glad that Finland had the True Finns Party.

'Oh,' I said, crestfallen, 'and it was going so well ...'

'No,' he pleaded. 'You don't understand. We have proportional representation. We can corral all the nutters in one place, and let them have their say, but they don't poison the rest of the electorate like ... ' He coughed in mild embarrassment. 'Like in Britain.'

And then, of course, there are those people whose homeland is also Finland, and was indeed before there was a Finland to speak of. Today there remain some 10,000 Saami in Finland, mainly in Lapland. As has been the case for a thousand years, the most visible ones are the ones who continue to herd reindeer, although the herding of reindeer has been rendered increasingly difficult by the construction of roads, dams, and international borders. The Finnish right wing is regularly animated into annoyance by the 'concessions' made to Saami politicians – restrictions on mining and forestry in the far north, designed to preserve the dwindling reindeer ranges. Such policies, however, do not go far enough for the Saami, who continue to protest that their *siida* way of semi-nomadic life, in not being officially recognised by the state, continues to be buffeted by political forces. The closure of the national borders, for example, mid-COVID pandemic, led to a legal limbo in the far north, where reindeer did not recognise such ephemeral restrictions. Nor were the Saami happy about the Finnish state's willingness to grant mineral exploitation rights to a Dutch mining company in Enontekiö, one of the last areas of the country where Saami reindeer herds had free range. Finland had voted in support of the 2007 United Nations Declaration on the Rights of Indigenous Peoples, noted the president of the Saami Council, Christina Hendriksen, 'but still has not recognised the rights of the Saami people.'

It was, in fact, a matter of some surprise to me that I could become a Finnish citizen through proving language proficiency in Finnish, in Swedish, or even in sign-language for the deaf, but not in Saami. In Finland's far north, they remain an unanswered question, and something of a contradiction, a people who wish to be left alone, but are also integral to the region's tourist appeal. The way in which their homeland denies modern borders is summed up by their anthem, written by the Norwegian Saami politician Isak Saba in 1906, and translated into seven different Saami languages. After a verse describing the region in blunt geographical terms, and two further verses outlining local colour in winters and summers, the song gets down to history and the future:

> Saamiland's people
> With unbending strength
> Defeated killing enemies, bad trades,
> Sly and evil thieves.
> Hail thee, tough Saami kin!
> Hail thee, root of freedom!
> Never was there battle,
> Never brother's blood was spilt
> Amongst the peaceful Saami kin.
>
> Our ancestors long ago
> Trouble makers did defeat.
> Let us, brothers, also resist
> Staunchly our oppressors.
> Oh, tough kin of the sun's sons,
> Never shall you be subdued
> If you heed your golden Saami tongue,
> Remember the ancestors' words.
> Saamiland for the Saami!

Centenary, COVID and NATO

In 2017, Finland celebrated the centenary of its republic, in a year-long series of events, matched by many kindly gestures from other nations. In Rio de Janeiro, Brazil, the statue of Christ the Redeemer was lit up in blue and white, as were the waters of Canada's Niagara Falls and Mexico City's Angel of Independence. Back in Finland a massive nationwide singing event, including an online performance by a choir of thousands, made Sibelius' 'Finlandia' hymn the song of the day, alongside a bafflingly with-it proclamation from the president's office that karaoke bars around the land should all focus on nothing but Finnish golden oldies.

In a touching social media campaign, the people of Norway tried to persuade their government to give Finland something it lacked, by nudging their border a crucial twenty metres so that Mount Halti would be on Finnish territory, and Finland, a land of fells but no official mountains, would finally have a peak of its own. Despite 17,000 supporters, the scheme was quashed by the Norwegian prime minister, reminding her citizens that the country's 1814 constitution proclaimed Norway 'indivisible', and hence they were unable to hand over a single inch of territory to anyone else. Norway promised instead to give something 'suitable', which was apparently a sculpture.

Undaunted, the Finnish president Sauli Niinistö gave a proud speech on New Year's Day 2018.

'The clear message of the centenary year,' he said, 'was that Finland's course has been successful, and that this is a good path to take into the future. The theme of the centenary year was "together"; this was seen as the secret of our success, and also the key to our future.'

However, the future was put on hold in 2020, for Finland and the rest of the world, with the outbreak of the COVID-19 pandemic. It came to Finland relatively early, on 29 January, when a Chinese tourist from Wuhan tested positive in Ivalo, Lapland. A Finnish woman returning from Milan in February was the next known case, with confirmed cases jumping to fifty in Helsinki by mid-March.

The Finnish reaction was cool-headed and swift. Borders were shut down in an Emergency Powers Act, Helsinki itself was effectively walled off from the rest of the country, travel was restricted, and schools were suspended for over a month. The country made it through with 1.2 million confirmed cases and 5,467 deaths. The period was not without its controversies, most notably a PPE supply scam in which a government minister was involved in the purchasing of millions of euros worth of medical masks that turned out to be unfit for purpose. The Finnish economy contracted by 6.2% before it began to rise again, with travel, tourism, and hospitality the hardest-hit industries. In one unexpected revelation, the Finnish liquor industry suffered a strong hit, since it turned out that much of its biggest profits had been in airport sales. But it was also a time in which Finns could be proud of their level reaction and stoic behaviour – the supply chains never really lapsed, public services continued to function, and although nobody was all that pleased about weeks of home-schooling with the playgrounds and swimming pools shut down, Finland made it through. My enduring memory of the period is that of the Finnish prime minister Sanna Marin, only a couple of months into her term of office, presenting a press conference for Finnish children in which she tried to explain to seven-year-olds why the adults were all behaving so weirdly.

The country's youngest ever prime minister, sworn in aged thirty-four, Marin is deservedly an icon of modern Finland. Her appearance and demeanour certainly rattled much of the old guard, including the seventy-year-old Estonian minister of the interior, who mocked her confirmation as the installation of a 'sales girl' as a national leader. He was swiftly made to apologise, although most Finns of my acquaintance were not even sure why it was an insult and not a statement of all that was great and good about Finnish society. They remained justly proud that Finland was a country where a child from a broken home, raised by two lesbians, could work a cash register in a shop as a teenager and still be supported and cherished by a welfare system that would propel her to a master's degree in political science. Marin was the far-right's worst nightmare – a vegetarian 'unwed mother' (she married the father of her child a year or so after taking office, sixteen years into their relationship) who wore leather jackets to rock concerts and danced at night clubs. She also came to power at the head of a coalition of parties, four out of five leaders of which were fellow millennial women under thirty-five. The German magazine *Bild* called her the 'coolest politician in the world'.

Marin had only just steered the country through COVID when Finland faced a new issue, the greatest political question since the referendum on joining the European Union. The Russian invasion of Ukraine in 2022 raked Finland over the coals of its long and tense relationship with the state on its eastern frontier, and propelled the Finnish government into consideration of a question that had been impossible to ask during the Cold War. Should Finland join NATO?

The answer had always previously been no. Studiously avoiding the North Atlantic Treaty Organisation in the years of Kekkonen had allowed Finland to avoid being dragged into the Warsaw Pact. But now there was no Warsaw Pact, and both the European Union and NATO with it were marching steadily eastwards.

The issue in the twenty-first century had retained shadows of Kekkonen's old arguments. Finland should avoid antagonising Russia by not forming any defence deals with NATO. This would seem to have been borne out by the Ukraine experience, with Russia invading shortly after Ukraine refused to back down on a decision to apply for membership. Finnish political pundits rued a lost opportunity – Russia had barely lifted a finger when Estonia joined NATO in 2004, and that would have been the time for Finland to get away with it. But Ukraine was somehow a sea change in Finnish thinking, with national polls swinging in a matter of weeks from resisting NATO's advances to signing up right away.

In part, the Finnish reaction was bolstered by the rhetoric coming out of Moscow, where the Russian premiere Vladimir Putin questioned Ukraine's right to exist as a state at all, and openly whipped up the cheap seats with speculations about reuniting *all* the pieces of Russia's empire under the tsars. In more recent times, there has been a surfeit of 'Georgian' restaurants in Helsinki, which are sometimes genuine, but also a discreet way for Russian businesses to keep their head down. For the same reason, my favourite

Russian restaurant in the capital has recently started flying a prominent Ukrainian flag outside its front door.

This was all tied into the perceived threat from Russia. Having attacked Georgia in 2008 and gobbled up Crimea in 2014, its 2022 'special operation' in Ukraine sent tanks and soldiers into the Donbas region. After decades of careful brinkmanship, the Finns proclaimed that enough was enough, and that there seemed no point in trying to avoid antagonising the Russians by joining NATO. If Russia was going to be antagonistic anyway, then Finland would throw away its previous caution, and align itself more firmly with other western powers.

One of the great joys of living in Finland in the 2010s had, until very recently, been the opportunity afforded by the trains that could whisk travellers away in a mere three hours across the lost lands of Karelia, and into the 'Finland Station' in the glittering St Petersburg, one of my favourite cities in the world, dedicated to pretending that the twentieth century never happened. There was, too, a long and lucrative commercial communication along that line, with St Petersburg, in particular, forming a mirror-self to Finland, a metropolis with a population equivalent to that of Finland itself, within commuting distance, dripping with opportunities.

As tensions over the Russian invasion of Ukraine increased worldwide, the train route between Helsinki and St Petersburg took on a new, portentous significance. The closure of airspace over Europe briefly turned the St Petersburg train into one of the only passenger routes into, or more appositely *out of*, Russia. In the weeks before it, too, was shut down by sanctions in March 2022, the train was packed to capacity with Russians fleeing Putin's regime. Before long, the car park at Helsinki airport was crowded with cars bearing Russian numberplates, as new arrivals sought to squeeze the last dregs from any Schengen visas, by driving to Finland and then taking a plane anywhere that would have them. They did so by driving through Finland, a country where Ilkka 'Frederik' Sysimetsä, the 'king of redneck disco', could still be found at local night clubs, belting out his taunting protest song 'Night Wolves', about Putin and his long-term mistress, Alina Kabaeva.

> The barrel of a cannon makes him feel bigger
> The rainbow boys get busted
> And, riding a tank, he demands votes
> All to gain more land.
> [...]
>
> He robs the people with the oligarchs
> And Alina gets a golden dacha
> Now a black belt *judoka* is leading the gang
> [...]
>
> The love of the Siberian bear burns like fire
> And the Empress gets her rubies.
> Tables loaded with champagne and caviar
> While the people just get cabbage.

In May that year, Prime Minister Sanna Marin and President Sauli Niinistö jointly announced that Finland would be seeking NATO membership, a decision backed by an overwhelming cross-party majority in the Finnish parliament. In pre-retaliation for something Finland had yet to do, Putin shut down the gas supply – a move which the Finns greeted with studied indifference. The shortfall was easily taken up elsewhere, not the least because the long-delayed Olkiluoto third reactor was just about to come online. I waited, with bated breath, for the Finnish media to mention this rather important fact, but it remained largely unreported, quite possibly because the usually stoic Finns were laughing their heads off behind closed doors. In an age of power-supply bullying, perhaps their nuclear capability didn't look like such a silly idea after all.

The likelihood of a Russian squeeze on Finnish resources had been something that the Finns had expected for a long while, not least because it was the subject of a 2015 science fiction novel by Ilkka Remes, Finland's best-selling author for the first two decades of the twenty-first century. Remes excelled at imagining worst-case scenarios in which Russia created problems for the state on its doorstep, for example in his novel *Jäätyvä helvetti* ('Frozen Hell'), in which Russia shuts the country down by simply cutting off its power supply.

Unlike some European states, deeply in hock to Russia just to keep the lights on, Finland was sitting on a viable alternative. In June, the *Monument to Selfishness* in Helsinki was altered with a can of red spray paint by unknown vandals, who daubed a contradictory slogan right across it: '*YDIN VOIMA PELASTAA ILTIASTON*' ('Nuclear power saves the night').

Ben Zyscowicz, a member of the Finnish parliament whose name is one of those carved on the slab, commented to the *Helsingin Sanomat* that changes in the political situation had radically altered the monument's meaning, and that he now considered the presence of his name on the list to be an honour and a vindication.

According to Zyskowicz, the monument should not be destroyed or moved from its place, because 'it tells about its own time'. 'The monument is always a timely reminder of the stupidity of those who opposed nuclear power.' In Zyskowicz's opinion, the monument has turned against the erectors. According to him, the builders should ask themselves 'what state the electricity supply would be in next winter if Olkiluoto had not been voted on then'.

Sini Harkka, the Nordic Programme Director for Greenpeace, replied with eye-rolling patience that the same amount of money could just as easily have been put into wind power, with swifter returns, but for a while, at least, it seemed that a greater, more immediate threat was dampening the Finns' traditional ardour for green issues.

In Helsinki in the autumn of 2022, putting the final touches to this book, I walked down to Senaatintori to look in on the statue of Alexander II, the 'Good Tsar', still quietly celebrated by the Finns as a representative of all that was good about their time as imperial subjects, before the double-headed eagle started hassling that girl on the figurative beach. At the base of Alexander's plinth, anonymous well-wishers had left more flowers than ever.

There will be more statues. There will be more songs. Finland in the twenty-first century is a vibrant parliamentary democracy, a modern republic, and a state deeply enmeshed in the new Europe. The question of what constitutes 'Finnishness' remains as debatable as always, ever since that legendary medieval day on a frozen lake, when a man struck a bishop with an axe and began the story of Finland.

8

Echoes of the Past

'Can you imagine, when I was in Finland, they took me to see an eighteenth-century wooden church,' scoffed Silvio Berlusconi, the gaffe-prone Italian prime minister. 'I remember how important this was to them. We woke up early in the morning and travelled to the church for three hours. Over here such a church would have been bulldozed to the ground.'

He was referring to the UNESCO World Heritage Site at Petäjävesi, a fascinating stave church built in a matter of weeks by local carpenters in the 1760s, using materials from several old barns nearby. It stands today as one of the sole surviving representatives of what was once a common style and architecture, its beams impressively wide, from the days when trees grew *really* big in unspoilt forests, its decorations spartan and quaintly simple. When first completed, it had no altarpiece, but instead a large window that looked out on to the lake beyond – a quasi-pagan call to the natural world. A century later, the window was covered over with a painted altarpiece by a wandering artist who sold his services to outlying parishes. The scene is of the Last Supper, the disciples rapt in attention as Jesus says grace over the wine, all except for Judas Iscariot, his head propped up on his left fist, who stares out sadly and resentfully at the viewer, mulling over the betrayal about to come.

The church at Petäjävesi is a wonderful glimpse of Finland's past, and a doleful reminder of the centuries of struggle and gumption that carried the Finns to their prosperous modern world. Berlusconi's aghast reaction is repeated here for the awful image it presents of southern European dignitaries' unrealistic expectations, and the Finns' earnest but vain efforts to impress them. It was, of course, gauche and inconsiderate of Berlusconi to expect objects in Finland of a similar culture and type to those he is used to in his ruin-clogged homeland. Finland's harsh environment and harsher recent history have destroyed many stone buildings and ancient relics, but it is helpful to recall that much of Finland's appeal, ever since the first travellers arrived on a Grand Tour, has been its unspoilt nature.

Berlusconi will never be able to look up into Italian night skies, as visitors to Lapland can so often do, and see the ghostly green river of the Aurora Borealis shimmering in the crisp air, making castles of light and sparkling wild hunts of phantoms. He cannot trudge through an Italian forest that stretches for hundreds of miles, or jet-ski a whole eighteen-hour day along the coasts of a lake that cuts through the middle of his country. It is unlikely that he will enjoy the mad thrill of taking a shortcut to walk across a frozen river (although one presumes it is all too likely that he has, at some point, been whipped with birch twigs by a naked girl in a steamy room).

While the previous chapter deals with the onward march of history, this final section of the book deals with those echoes of the Finnish past that resound for the modern-day visitor, and which cause the historian to pause, quite often in the street, when someone is chivvying him along somewhere else. Steep yourself for long enough in Finland and Finnishness, and it starts to speak to you from the oddest of places – street signs, statues, and trademarks among other things.

The Metadata of Meals

Finnish food achieved international notoriety in 2005 when Silvio Berlusconi, that one-man anti-Finland missile, proclaimed that it was awful, and the Finns a bunch of philistines who 'don't even know what Parma ham is'. With matching charm, France's former president Jacques Chirac later agreed, observing sagely that it was even worse than English food – itself a running joke in Europe ever since Olaf the Stout chuckled at King Canute being stuck in Cabbage-land.

The Finnish food industry fought back with what, for Finns, was a stinging rebuke, although Berlusconi might well have countered that they had made his point for him. A red onion, mushroom, and smoked reindeer pizza, known as 'the Berlusconi', went on to win the 2008 New York Pizza Show, beating Italy into second place.

Many international restaurant critics also sprung to Finland's defence, citing superb, world-class meals eaten in Finnish restaurants. Since 2011, Finland has also been the epicentre of the International Restaurant Day (*ravintolapäivä*), when on pre-agreed dates, now several times a year, pop-up eateries spring to life on street corners and verandas. However, while it is true that good food does exist in Finland, we might timidly concede that Berlusconi could have been onto something.

Sitting down, or indeed standing up, to eat anywhere in Finland is a window into history past and present, a fascinating portal to Finnish culture – a remote, climatically compromised forest environment, reluctantly giving way to dairy and simple crops, tardily accepting a few exotica on import, and then enduring a late twentieth century partly walled off from many developments in modern foodways. Even the metadata – what's on sale or not on sale in the supermarkets, what's the new fad, what's the restaurant with a queue outside – can all offer glimpses of the Finnish past, and indeed the Swedish and Russian pasts.

As long as you are prepared to pay, not only is good food within your immediate grasp, almost anywhere in Finland outside the smallest village, but also the Finn who sells it to you will know appreciably more about its preparation and suitability than you do. The grade inflation caused by Finland's free education system has put immensely knowledgeable people into every sector of the food industry, from farmers to waiters, and it is entirely normal for your butcher to have a master's degree in meat technology, and for your grocer to be a postgraduate agronomist.

In the Finns' defence, the immense freshness of their locally sourced food, and the prospect offered by the natural winter temperature for refrigeration, may have combined to create a palate that avoids the spices and condiments of warmer countries. But Finnish cuisine has always had the odds stacked against it, with a short growing season, thin soil, and limited resources, so that even cattle need special protection. The Viking sagas marked one particularly harsh winter by wailing: 'Like the Finns have we our bud-eaters bound in barns.'

In part, the Russian era is also to blame, particularly for a culinary tradition that offered a table of free nibbles, while only expecting the patrons to pay for the vodka. A French chef in St Petersburg once gave Gustaf Mannerheim a tongue-lashing for knocking back tastebud-numbing schnapps at the beginning of a meal.

One also gets the sense among many Finns that food is still little more than fuel to many of them, best cheaply sourced and swiftly tanked. Perhaps as a relic of their hard-working, farming past and the likelihood of inclement, freezing weather outside, Finns are far more likely to have a hearty breakfast and all but ignore lunch, further reducing the opportunities for dining as a public, social occasion. Faced with a nice French meal for double the London price, or a crispbread and something from the salad bar, the average no-nonsense Finn is liable to go for the latter. Monty Python's hymn to 'a snack lunch in the hall' was presciently accurate, since there seems to be little acceptance of the more Mediterranean custom of time taken with multiple courses and conversation – Finns not being famed for the latter. There are also invisible undercurrents influencing Finnish dining, including the stipulation of the tax office that a deductible lunch is capped at a mere €11. In addition, the rival money-off programmes of the two supermarket chains S Group and K Group have effectively sewn up much of the Finnish high street and shopping centre. These loyalty schemes offer all sorts of perks, from free parking to free toilet access in affiliated stores, as well as discounted eating, all of which steers the average Finn in search of lunch towards a mega-mall full of chain restaurants, to the detriment of any finer or more localised dining.

The worst enemies of Finnish cuisine are the Finns themselves, an overwhelming majority of whom seem happy with all-you-can-eat buffets and tasteless dole. Moreover, the free healthcare system's willingness to categorize almost anything as a 'condition' has fostered a culture of needlessly fussy eaters. Many are the world-class, Michelin-worthy Finnish chefs and restaurateurs, I have observed, biting their lips and trying not to go crazy with a meat cleaver, as local diners ask them if it's possible to have the onion soup without any onions in it. A Thai restaurant in Jyväskylä, now sadly defunct, once placed a sign on every table that spoke of the cooks' recurring anguish with their unappreciative clientele. It read as follows:

We cook our food to Finnish standards.
If you want it done properly, let us know.

Try to interest a group of Finns in fine dining and listen in torment as one claims not to like 'foreign' food, and another regards anything above eight euros as too much to pay for lunch. Inevitably, they will then start comparing their alleged allergies and intolerances, and before you know it, you, too, will be muddling through at a pizza buffet in customary silence. But at least you've got some more points on your K-Plussa card, so you can save money on Persil. All of which amounts to a simple warning – there is great food to be had in Finland, but it is not cheap.

'The flavour of our cheeses has been much praised,' claimed Daniel Juslenius in 1700, although the author has found no evidence to back this up. Finnish cuisine favours forest products and game – mushroom soups and reindeer stew.

'We have one special dish which is not found elsewhere,' writes Juslenius with evident pride. 'It is made by boiling rye malt and, after placing it in a birch basket, baking it like bread in an oven. This food is dark but extremely sweet. It is called *mämmi*, and it is eaten on Easter Day in memory of unleavened bread.' Finns often seem to regard eating *mämmi* as some sort of test of endurance for tourists; accept the challenge, since it tastes like nothing so unusual as liquidised malt loaf.

Finns also seem oddly proud of the *kalakukko*, a fish baked inside a loaf of bread, which unfortunately translates into English as 'fish-cock'. Particularly famed as a local delicacy in Kuopio, this led to the odd situation in which the namesake express train from Helsinki, and the 1951 song about its delights, make it sound like someone is losing their mind.

The driver's whistle blows its air, releasing silver vapour
Shining on the tracks in its berth, the Flying
    Fish-Cock!
[...]
Keeping the worries and joys of the journey, the Flying
    Fish-Cock

181

The wheels lash out and 'We're on the road to Kuopio!'
The rails yell in reply: 'Off we go!'

Another widespread Finnish food is the Karelian pie (*Karjalan piirakka*, itself a loanword from the Russian *pirog*), an unassuming open-topped rye pasty, which along with the unremarkable Karelian stew evokes memories of the lost lands on many a kitchen table. The worst of them taste like cardboard; the best taste of nothing, but are supposed to be rendered edible with a generous spread of eggy butter (*munavoi*), usually to be found close at hand. These are relatively common in hotel buffets, and may form your first encounter with genuinely Finnish food.

Otherwise, Finnish chefs often try a little bit too hard to incorporate that nebulous sense of 'Finnishness' into other dishes, and default to garnishing everything with berries. The lingonberry, huckleberry, and cloud berry are particular favourites, but the Finns have almost as many berries in their repertoire as allergies, and are sure to sneak a few into your food if you are not looking.

The Swedish era left its mark with several regional cuisines and customs, particularly the orgy of crustacean abuse that arrives each year with the crayfish season. Finnish salmon, i.e. gravlax, is excellent, as are any other lake- or Baltic-sourced marine dishes you are liable to encounter. As in Sweden, pea soup (*hernekeitto*) is served on Thursdays, with a dash of mustard to give it some zing. This tradition continues in the military, where the ease of preparing it in bulk is appreciated, and often crosses over into public life for the same reason, with pea soup forming a staple part of Finnish school dinners, and even handed out by the mugful by tub-thumping politicians cultivating an image of homespun approachability. If my late father-in-law had his way, my own wedding would have ended with a barrel of pea soup in the forest, thereby making it possible to invite everybody in Central Finland.

The forensically minded can have a lot of fun trying to work out which foreign food is being approximated with Finnish ingredients. 'Swedish' meatballs, for example, seem to be distant facsimiles of the Greek *kieftedes*, picked up on the edges of the Ottoman Empire by King Karl XII during his Moldavian exile. There is also a Finnish meatball – the sauce is different – although the only place I have ever seen Finns eat them is in the dining car on the train to St Petersburg, where they defiantly order them the moment the train is over the border.

The Russian century's influence has waned on main courses, although Finnish supermarkets still do a brisk trade in Smetana sour cream and *pasha*, a delightfully rich Easter custard – the Russian name was originally *paskha*, but unfortunately that is a homonym in Finnish for excrement. One other odd legacy of the Tsar's empire is *vorschmack*, a salty meat dish of mashed herrings, onions, and offal, served with pickles and sour cream, a delicacy brought back to Finland by Gustaf Mannerheim after his service as a regimental commander in Poland. This tall tale is so well established that the leading brand is Marskin Vorschmack ('the Marshal's Vorschmack'), but beyond that, you are on your own. It looks so repulsive that I have not been able to bring myself to ever try it.

Spend any time dining with Finns, and you may notice that much of their apparent disinterest in food evaporates when dessert comes around. The average Finn, it seems, will happily gargle sawdust and gnaw on iron filings as long as there is ice cream for afters. Finnish ice cream, eaten all year round, even in winter, is an unexpectedly classy affair, coming in many excellent flavours, including the rare variants of liquorice, *terva* ('wood tar'), and the salty *salmiakki* ('ammonium chloride'). The Finns are also hugely proud of their cakes, buns, and tarts, none of which seem remotely remarkable.

During the Cold War, it was often said that the world's best Russian food could be found in Helsinki, and the capital remains an epicurean delight. Particularly in the centre, it offers fine selections of international cuisine, as well as high-class dining in the European style. Outside the capital, fine dining opportunities decline, and the visitor to most other Finnish cities is liable to exhaust the opportunities to try new restaurants in the average weekend.

Finland did not get its first pizzeria until 1969, although the modern visitor would be forgiven for thinking it was the national dish. Local additions like reindeer and chanterelle mushrooms add a dash of variety to Finnish pizzas, and you can be sure to find someone ready to rustle up a Berlusconi.

Much fast food outside the usual chains and the local Hesburger cafés seems to be in the hands of hard-working Turks and Eastern European immigrants, who are doing their level best to establish the kebab as a staple food.

One chain worthy of note is Harald, a 'Viking' restaurant

that deftly avoids reminding diners that Vikings didn't actually come from Finland, although they might have occasionally robbed it. There are currently eight branches across the country from Helsinki to Oulu. Although the cuisine is mainly modern, it tends towards ingredients that would have been available in the Middle Ages, and has a mead-hall ambience that is sure to include your steak being delivered on the point of a sword, a cheese board served on a piece of longship oar, and fellow diners donning historically inaccurate but always entertaining horned helmets. It'll look better on Instagram than yet another picture of you shovelling a cheesecake into your face.

From Temperance to Pantsdrunk

It's when the Finns drink that their non-European origins become most obvious, not least at the average Finnish breakfast table, where one brand of milk is never enough. The baffled visitor will often encounter pasteurised milk, skimmed milk, semi-skimmed milk, fat-free milk, cream, coffee cream, sour milk, fortified milk, and usually also a lactose-free, fat-free, milk-free milk so removed from everyday cow juice that European Union food regulations insisted its name be changed to Milk Drink (*maitojuoma*).

That's before you get to the yoghurts. One senses here the distant undercurrent of Finland's past, when a nation of dairy farmers tried boldly to pretend they weren't all carrying lactose-intolerant Asian genes, or perhaps an indicator of Finns' habitual hypochondria, where everybody needs to feel special, even when putting something on their cornflakes. Marry a Finn, and doom yourself to endless arguments about precisely what kind of milk someone meant by putting the lone word on the shopping list.

And then there is that other gene, the one that has trouble breaking down alcohol. In spite of this, Finns have always been legendary drinkers, such that Elias Lönnrot, on his posting to Kajaani, was dumbfounded at what passed for abstinence – only consuming hard liquor with meals, and once every couple of hours.

Said Voltaire of the Finns in 1731:

> The climate is severe; there is scarcely any spring or
> autumn, but there are nine months of winter in the
> year ... The people ... live to a good old age when
> they do not undermine their constitutions by the
> abuse of strong drink, which northern nations seem
> to crave all the more because they have been denied
> them by Nature.

Perhaps understandably, the country also enjoyed a strong temperance movement. An entire voting bloc of exasperated womenfolk flooded the ballots after independence and voted in Prohibition (*Kieltolaki*), which lasted from 1919 to 1932. As in America, this led to a culture of secret drinking, 'fortified' teas and cross-border bootlegging. Booze was sneaked in from Tallinn and Danzig (Russia and Sweden, each for different reasons, not offering much of a supply), and by the 1920s, 80% of reported Finnish 'crime' was linked to the supply or consumption of alcohol. The authorities were woefully under-equipped to police such a huge boom in illegal behaviour, leaving them overwhelmed. In 1930, one year's confiscated alcohol amounted to over a million litres. A 1931 referendum voted by a vast majority to repeal the law, but its echoes endure.

Alcohol in Finland remains prohibitively expensive, subject to the guilt tax common to Nordic countries. Harder liquor (over 5.5% ABV) and wines are only available from the government-run off-licences, which are called Alko without a scrap of irony – it is short for Alkoholiliike, or State Alcohol Monopoly. As with Finnish restaurants, these establishments are usually staffed by ridiculously knowledgeable and experienced connoisseurs, gritting their teeth as they have to ID yet another trio of giggling teenagers trying to buy three litres of cider.

Far from discouraging drinking among the Finns, such obstacles have backfired in many cases, fostering an environment that encourages binge drinking and surreptitious under-the-table tipples. Many otherwise-educated Finnish youths barely encounter alcohol before their twenties, and then have no clue how to use it responsibly. The German tradition of copious, extremely light beer strikes the Finn as a waste of time and effort (alcohol content below 2% remained legal during Finnish Prohibition, and apparently wasn't good enough). Do not be surprised if you hear Finns speaking of a pre-party or a continuation-party, referring to a booze-up in a private home to get properly munted, as opposed to the official public gathering in a bar or club, where nobody can afford to buy too many drinks. As in other Nordic countries, the concept of 'getting a round in' is regarded as an alien extravagance. When the time came for a set of specifically Finnish emojis for the cellphone generation, one of the approved icons was *kalsarikännit* or 'pantsdrunk' – getting drunk in one's underwear, with no intention of leaving the house.

Many Finnish establishments conflate multiple styles of bar into a single venue. It is often possible to walk into a French-style coffee bar (which also serves alcohol – a tobacco-free *tabac*), and pass through inner doors into a snug facsimile of a British pub, and then through further doors to a riotous American-style dive bar (called in Finnish a *räkälä*, or 'place of snot').

Do not be surprised if a passive-aggressive temperance afflicts staff in some restaurants, such as the waitress in Jyväskylä who once asked the author if he 'was sure' he wanted a second beer at lunch. I also report the following guessing game, verbatim, from one of Tampere's best-known hotels.

> 'And what would sir like to drink?'
>
> 'There are no beers on the menu. Presumably you have some?'
>
> 'We've got all of them.'
>
> 'Fine, I'll have a Guinness.'
>
> 'We haven't got that.'
>
> 'A Lapin Kulta?'
>
> 'We haven't got that, either.'

Despite such obstructions, the visitor is liable to encounter several Finnish beers, whose stories are often more worthy of attention than their flavours. Common brands include Lapin Kulta ('Gold of Lapland', or 'Lapland Darling'), which alludes to the Finnish gold rush of the 1870s, but takes its name from its original brewery in Tornio, although now it is only brewed far to the south; Karhu ('Bear'), and Koff (short for the brewer's name, Sinebrychoff). Look out for some odder names, such as Olvi's grab for the military market with Tuntematon Sotilas ('the Unknown Soldier', named for Väinö Linna's novel), and Sandels, named for Count Johan August Sandels (1764–1831), who led Swedish troops to victory against the Russians – he won the battle, but lost the war. History also comes to the fore with Karjala (Karelia), which uses the coat of arms of Karelia as its logo. This presents the armoured sword-arm of a European knight striking a blow against a scimitar-wielding Asian. The brand was losing market share until the 1960s, when the Soviet ambassador complained that it evoked echoes of the Winter War. Finns immediately began quaffing it in great quantities. The Laitila brewery produces a variety of ales, including the pointlessly strong Imperiaali, a black, gloopy poison at 9.2%, adorned with a double-headed rooster, spoofing the Tsar's crest of old. Other common beers in Finland include Estonian brands such as A. le Coq and Saku.

European Union regulations decree that Finnish grain alcohols be termed vodka, although locally the Russian word is usually only applied to imported liquors. Locally, grain alcohol is often called *viina*, or in Swedish, *bränvinn*. The most famous brand is Koskenkorva (or more affectionately, Kossu), which forms the basis of many modern, quaintly bonkers Finnish cocktails. These include the Kossukola (with Coke), the Kossu Battery (with an energy drink), and the Fisu (with crushed Fisherman's Friend cough lozenges).

Particularly popular among visitors, and sold in ready-made bottles, is Salmiakki Koskenkorva (popularly nick-named Salmiakki Kossu or Salmari), which combines a famous local *viina* with Turkish Pepper flavouring. The result is a jet-black vodka that tastes of liquorice. It makes for a fine souvenir, although the appeal soon wears off – many are the enthusiastic converts who never finish the bottle they bring home.

Among unique Finnish tipples, the historically minded traveller's attention is drawn to Marskin Ryyppy ('the Mar-shal's Schnapps'), a mixture of strong alcohol, vermouth, and a touch of gin, allegedly concocted by Mannerheim's adjutant during the Winter War as a means of coping with low-quality rotgut. It smells and tastes like a mad scientist has been trying to recreate a vodka martini in a lab, and is served judderingly ice-cold in shots. The glasses are customarily filled to overflowing, so that a meniscus of alcohol peaks over the top. Depending on who you ask, this is either a relic of the Russian Chevalier Guard, who wanted to ensure their mandated single shot a day had the maximum content, or of Mannerheim's wartime custom of watching his officers as they drank, and furloughing anyone whose jangled nerves led them to spill a drop.

Finland's other claim to fame (or infamy) in the alcohol stakes came into being in 1952, when the country was barely a generation out of Prohibition, but facing the prospect of a vast influx of foreign tourists coming to the Helsinki Olym-pics. Enterprising bar owners, pressed for storage space and disposal logistics, hit on the idea of mixing vats of hard liquor with gallons of flavoured soda, in order to make bulk quantities of what might be termed alcopops in other countries. In Finland they were known as 'long drinks', popularly shortened to *lonkero*, which literally means 'tentacle'. The most popular brand dilutes perfectly good gin with acrid, sharp grapefruit juice – as with the Marskin Ryypy, it seems like an imitation, in this case as if an infant school had been left in charge of creating a facsimile of a gin and tonic. The author is baffled, and eternally exasperated, as to why Finland didn't just mix the gin with tonic.

Finland has taken several hesitant steps into the world of whisky, although currently it is more of a waiting game. Panimoravintola Beer Hunters in Pori is waiting for its first malt casks to mature in 2034, while Panimoravintola Koulu in Turku released a three-year-old malt in 2013. Teerenpeli's six-year-old single malt was released in Lahti in 2009 – every bottle comes with a free wooden coaster, as well it might at €70 for half a litre.

National Holidays and Local Festivals

Finnish national holidays reflect those of the Christian world, with occasional oddities left over from the distant pagan past. The Finnish Easter retains elements of the country's Russian past, as well as traditions from pagan and Orthodox Karelia. The gap between Good Friday and Easter Sunday is supposedly the point in the year where God's power is weakest, leading to many legends of witches and trolls. In a custom not dissimilar to trick-or-treating, children are apt to go door-to-door dressed as witches and waving twigs as wands, chanting a spell in Finnish so archaic that it is practically Estonian:

Virvon, varvon
tuoreeks terveeks,
tulevaks vuodeks,
ison talon emännäks.
Vitsa sulle,
palkka mulle.

In the unlikely event you are confronted with such a super-natural assault on your visit to Finland, you may rest easy – the words imply prosperity, and long life is assured to the 'warden of the big house' if you bribe them with sweets. If you do not want a nice house and long life, slam the door in their face and face sorcerous consequences.

The Nordic summer is notoriously short, and the Finns, like other northern races, are aggressively keen to wring the most out of it as possible. Finns go certifiably mental on the evening of 30 April and day of 1 May (Walpurgisnacht, or *Vappu* in Finnish), in what is officially a series of ceremonies to mark Labour Day, but usually little more than an excuse for a party. The more genteel Finns will picnic in the park and sip on low-alcohol mead. But the day really belongs to the students, who are liable to rampage through town centres wearing boilersuits festooned with sponsor patches. Anyone who has graduated from a Finnish high school dons their white graduation cap on this day, which makes many Finnish towns look like they have been over-run with sailors. The celebrations officially begin at 6 p.m. on 30 April, when one such cap will be jauntily placed on the head of the statue of Havis Amanda, a statue of the Spirit of Love in Helsinki, that at the time of its unveiling was regarded as a scandalous image of a teenage French nude, but now is adopted by the Finnish youth as one of them.

As with Vappu in the spring, Finland's midsummer celebration of St John's Eve on 22 June has less to do with any prosaic or modern events, and owes more to an atavistic, primal celebration of summer itself. Its origins seem to date back to the pagan festival of Ukko, the chief god of Finland's pantheon, who was worshipped with great pyres.

Finns are liable to run to the countryside in summer anyway, and will be all the more absent from town centres on this day – it usually amounts to a three-line whip for family gatherings, analogous to the American Thanksgiving, and often seems to exert more of a gravitational pull than even Christmas.

Finns are deeply proud of their summer cottages (though you should not dare make the obvious comparison to Russian *dachas*), and midsummer is arguably the best time to experience them, swimming in a lake after a wood-fired sauna, beneath a never-ending sunset. Finns frolic in the woods, get drunker than usual, and light massive bonfires.

The plastic-pumpkin Americanised Halloween is slowly destroying any uniquely Finnish traditions. The more devout Finns will scurry to the local cemetery and place windproof candles on the graves of relatives and friends. Particularly on the nearest Saturday to Halloween, the lit graveyards can look hauntingly beautiful in the autumn darkness. Some Finnish farm towns used to assemble a ram effigy in fir or wicker branches, dragging it through the streets and burning it (sometimes on a nearby lake) on All Saint's Day as a form of post-harvest festival. Known as a

Kekripukki, the name literally means 'relict ram', although early Christian commentators suggested that Kekri was a homonym for a forgotten fertility god, and also a term for the end of the agricultural year. Kekripukki celebrations, which also included mummery, costumed antics, and wassailing, were viewed as deeply suspect by the early Church. Its siting on All Saints' Day appears to have been a Christian attempt to incorporate it within the Church year, whereas different locales previously held their celebrations on slightly different autumn dates. The tradition faded out in modern times, lingering for a while in Eastern Finland. Modern Kekripukki celebrations can still be found in Oulu and Kajaani.

Like many Europeans, the Finns celebrate Christmas on the night before Christmas Day, which they call Joulu, cognate with the Norse Yule. Santa Claus (Joulupukki) may put in a live appearance, although he usually manages to arrive whenever Dad has popped out to the cornershop. As a result, the two of them are suspiciously rarely seen together – the alert visitor can often look out the window and see several Santas at once stumbling through the snow from house to house in the afternoon, as neighbours swap Santa responsibilities.

In what seems to be a relic of a Karelian smithy tradition, some Finns heat tin scraps and then fling the molten metal into a bucket of water. The flash-hardened residue is then examined for shapes, portents, images, and omens of the future. This will be what a Finn means when he tells you he has been at a party 'examining slags'.

Architecture and Public Art

There are other historical echoes to be found in Finnish public spaces, from the fortress-like National Romantic buildings that pepper Helsinki, to the Russian-era clapperboard houses of Turku and Pori. The ludicrously opulent Mail and Customs House at Eckerö on the Åland Islands is itself a glimpse of a different era – back when the islands were the westernmost point of the Tsar's empire, Alexander I deliberately arranged for them to put on a show of imperial grandeur for any approaching ships. The capital of Åland, Mariehamm, dervies its name from the wife of Alexander II, Marie of Hesse.

With typical Finnish self-awareness, the Suomen Kansallismuseo ('National Museum of Finland') in Helsinki is itself a museum exhibit, one wing of which is designed to look like a church, which stood it in good stead during the war, when its appearance may have warded off Russian bombers. It was also the site of some scuffles during the Finnish Revolution, and its front doors still proudly display the bullet holes shot in the windows, now preserved behind a second layer of glass. The lobby is decorated with frescoes depicting scenes from the *Kalevala*, painted by Akseli Gallen-Kallela, and that's before you've even bought your ticket!

Helsinki harbour is also the place to get the ferry to nearby Suomenlinna, the Fortress of Finland, which remains a quaint getaway for the marine minded. It evokes the Swedish, Russian, and Finnish eras with numerous installations, as well as a couple of military museums and the Vesikko, a WW2 submarine open to the public. Visitors can also poke around the fortifications, including the King's

Gate, built in 1752 as a sufficiently royal arrival point for Swedish rulers. Nearby inscriptions note that King Adolf Frederick laid the first stone here, while a sad, uncompleted plaque leaves the date blank for King Gustav's laying of the final stone (he never got around to it). Beneath a plaque announcing that these 'wolf islands' have been transformed into a fort for the Swedes, a second inscription intones these words: '*Eftervärld, stå här på egen botn, och lita icke på främmande hielp.*' It is a fine prophecy for the world that lay in wait for the Finns: 'Those that come after us, stand here on your own foundation, and trust not in foreign help.'

Named for the medieval Stone Sacristy (now a church museum) dedicated to the Archangel Michael at nearby Savilahti, Mikkeli enjoyed a long history as a trading post. The Suur-Savo Museum reconstructs the kind of costumes that might have been worn by the owners of twelfth-century jewellery dug up in nearby Tuukkala, presumably dating from the era of the first northern crusades. The wartime headquarters of the Finnish army, Mikkeli was heavily bombed as a result, and little of the pre-war town remains. The town celebrates its experience in its coat-of-arms, which today includes the crossed double batons of Gustaf Mannerheim and a Cross of Liberty medal. Mannerheim's Railway Carriage, which formed a mobile command post (and once, a dining car for Adolf Hitler) sits proudly but a little forlornly on the platform at the railway station. With peeling paint and grimy windows, it is protected by a roof from the rain but not the elements. It is open to visitors only once a year on Mannerheim's birthday, 4 June.

The elements and, latterly, the Lapland War of 1944–5

have ensured that there are few buildings more than eighty years old in Lapland. Rovaniemi has fought back with a passionately modernist engagement with the tourist trade, most famously with Santa Claus Village, a theme park that has single-handedly put the town on many international travellers' itineraries. The town achieved a more ephemeral fame as the home of Lordi, the cheerfully bombastic, grotesquely masked heavy metal band that swept to Eurovision glory in 2006, quite possibly as the result of pan-European student larks. Do not be surprised if you are treated to the band's anthem 'Hard Rock Hallelujah' at least once during your stay. Lordi fever veritably gripped Finland for a number of years, and led to the renaming of the town's central Sampo Square as Lordi's Square (Lordin aukio). The band members' handprints are preserved in cement here.

Savonlinna, 'the castle of Savo', takes its name from St Olaf's Castle (Olavinlinna), the northernmost extant castle of the medieval period, built in 1475 to defend new settlements in the east of Finland, and named Nyslott ('New Castle') in Swedish. With canny calculation, it is actually some way inland, protecting not the old border with Russia itself, but a vital communications nexus that any invading army would be sure to cross. Mrs Alec Tweedie stayed there in the 1890s, spending a night haunted by the ghosts of times past:

> Here was the hall of the knights, a long and dark
> chamber – so dark, in fact, that we wondered how
> any one had ever been able to see clearly in it. On
> all sides were rooms and pitch-black dungeons, for

at the time the Castle was built (1475) the powers-
that-were thought nothing of shutting people up in
dark little holes, where they left them to die, and the
Olavin Linna seems to have been particularly rich
in such choice chambers. From where we stood, a
few steps up a winding staircase led us to a big tower
containing a large round room, called the ladies'
drawing-room. The dames of that period certainly
had a glorious view all round for miles and miles
although they were far removed from the life going
on below. From this point of vantage we saw how
the Castle literally covered the whole of the rock,
and occupied a most commanding position where
three lakes met. As we wandered down again, we
chanced into a queer sort of chamber, wherein half
a dozen weird straggling trees struggled to exist. It
was almost dark; the storms of winter could rustle
through those blank windows, and the trees were
white, and gray, and sickly – more like phantoms
than real trees – so queer and withered and pale and
anaemic were their leaves, and yet they stood eight
or ten feet high, showing they had boldly struggled
for life.

The castle remains an impressive sight, its cold conditions reflected in roofed turrets with portholes instead of
crenels. Its chapel is notable in particular for a hagioscope
– a peephole through which uninvited outsiders could
watch a service without disturbing the congregation. This
is thought to reflect the presence of lepers in the family of

one of the architects. The castle and town come alive in July, when they host the Savonlinna Opera Festival, with international class performances in the courtyard.

Proudly describing itself as 'the Manchester of the North', Tampere is a hub of modern tourist sites, often steeped in its industrial past. The Finlayson company still produces local textiles, more likely to be found with a Marimekko or Moomin print in modern times. A stroll from the main train station takes in not only the main shopping street, but also the Hämeensilta bridge across the Tammer rapids – adorned with Wäinö Aaltonen's four statues of ancient life in the area: the *Hunter*, the *Finnish Maiden*, the *Tradesman*, and the *Tax Collector* – to the Central Square, which remains a charming example of National Romantic style. Built long after Finlayson had left Finland, and hence named for the company rather than the man, the Finlaysonin Palatsi (literally 'Finlayson's Palace') is an impressive mansion at the water's edge, commissioned by the factory-owning Nottbeck family in 1899. It was converted to a posh restaurant in the 1980s.

Tampere Cathedral is a typically Finnish oddity, designed in the National Romantic style by Lars Sonck (1870–1956), and decorated inside by the certifiably eccentric Hugo Simberg (1873–1917), whose frescoes included a 'Garden of Death', in which cowled skeletons tend roses, and the twelve apostles appear as naked little boys. A massive altarpiece depicts the resurrection of Lazarus, although it more closely resembles a man emerging from a sauna. Most famously of all, tucked away in a corner you will find 'The Wounded Angel', a depiction of a blindfolded, winged girl on a stretcher, being borne away by two sheepish boys, said to symbolise Finland's battered history stuck between Russia and Sweden.

Foreign visitors are spared any engagement with the city's violent upheavals in Finland's civil war, although there are still clues, such as the fact that the town's statue of Gustaf Mannerheim has been shoved unceremoniously into a distant forest clearing, rather than erected in the town centre.

Finland's former capital of Turku – the name of which may derive from 'Barter' (*turgu*) in Old Slavic, or possibly simply 'The Residence' (*Åbo*) in Old Swedish – has seethed in snooty resentment ever since the Russians relocated all the action to that glorified army camp, Helsinki. When its location on the south-western corner led unkind wags to call it 'the arse of Finland', the city tourist board fought back with an advertising campaign in which numerous celebrities exhorted viewers to 'Kiss my Turku'. All of which makes the city sound like some over-defensive urban ruin, and not the rather charming Hanseatic town it is. It remains a delightful cultural centre of 'Swedish Finland', boasting the medieval Turku Castle at the mouth of the Aura River.

Turku Cathedral also offers a glimpse of the medieval 'New Lands', much wrecked and rebuilt during numerous historical fires and remodellings, but still boasting the immense sarcophagus of Katarina Jagellonica, the Polish princess who brought a touch of class to the sixteenth-century regional centre. You will also find the grave of Samuel Cockburn, the Scottish mercenary who ended up as a local baron after loyal service to the Swedish crown.

Aboa Vetus (Latin for 'Old Turku'), is built directly over the archaeological ruins of the medieval town, boasting not only authentic glimpses of the Turku of 800 years ago, but also a sad-looking mummified cat, thought to have been accidentally trapped in an in-filled cellar.

Finishing with Finnish

And finally, the Finnish language itself, which remains a living, infuriating piece of history. The fact it is spoken at all is a living testament to Finnish nationalism and grit, as one-by-one so many of the aristocratic families of the nineteenth century 'Fennicised' their Swedish names to honour their new national identity.

A Finno-Ugric language very different to most others in Europe, Finnish has consonantal shifts, vowel mutations, and an unerring habit of dropping doubled consonants and spaces between words that can make even loanwords hard to see. Even a double cheeseburger gets put through the wringer, turning into the one-word tongue-twister *tupla-juustohampurilainen* – which is to say a *tupla* (mutated 'double' from English), *juusto* ('ost' from Swedish for cheese) and *Hampurilainen* – a person from Hamburg, which in Finnish is Hampuri, the final letter softening the g in the Swedish fashion. Once you know where to look for them, many Swedish loanwords can be picked out, as can terms from Russian like *tarina* ('story', from *starina*, 'olden times'), *toveri* ('mate', from *tovarisch*, 'comrade') and *porkkana* ('carrot', from *borkan*). French loanwords also abound, sometimes at one step removed, since both the Swedes and the Russians like to tart up their languages with a bit of Francophone sophistication, such *vitriini* ('vitrine', a glass case), *subretti* ('soubrette', a cheeky servant girl), and *kroissantti* ('croissant'). There are also numerous loanwords from Saami, although since these tend to be terms for things that only people in Lapland have a whole lot of use for, they tend not to enter everyday conversation. These include a huge number of terms for different types and ages of reindeer, as well as such oddities as *vuotkia* (to de-bark a pine tree), *naali* (an Arctic fox), and *paltsa* (a hairless spot on a parka).

English, too, can pop up in forms both obvious (such as *kapitalismi*, *trendi*, and *taksi*), as well as in calques that invent new terms from translating their English components, such as *jälkäpallo* ('football') and *kotisivu* ('homepage'). As the COVID lockdown began to bite in 2020 and I realised I needed a new headset for Zoom meetings, I made a complete fool of myself in the electronics megastore (Gigantti) by embarking on a two-minute Finnish-language oration about how I wanted a pair of headphones that also came with a microphone attached to a little arm so that I could talk and hear people online. Straight-faced, as Finns invariably are, the sales assistant said: 'Oh, you mean a *hedsetti.*'

It was early on in my Finnish language-learning that I asked my teacher the ultimate question, which was how many words the Finnish language has for snow.

She fixed me with her big, blinky eyes, and sighed.

'No, you poor deluded fool,' she said. 'We Finns only have one word for "snow". The trouble is, you English think that everything white that falls out of the sky is "snow".'

Finnish actually has more than thirty words for frozen precipitation in a variety of forms, including a word for 'powdery snow that's melted just a little bit' (*nuoska*), a 'thin bit of snow on top of ice' (*iljanne*), and even 'the grey lumpy stuff that turns up when slush refreezes' (*kohva*). It is as one might expect for a language that naturally retains vestiges of an ancient past on icy fells beneath the Northern Lights, ever watchful against the ultimate enemy, the cold.

Chronology of Major Events

1150	Supposed date of the legendary and probably fictional First Swedish Crusade in Finland.
1153	The English Cardinal Nicholas Breakspear is a missionary in Finland in the company of the Swedes.
1154	Nicholas Breakspear becomes Pope Adrian IV.
1155	Supposed date of the martyrdom of Saint Henry, murdered by Lalli the Finn.
1172	Pope Alexander III complains that Finnish Christians are lax in their devotions.
1220	The Englishman Thomas is appointed first Bishop of Finland.
1237	Pope Gregory IX suggests a crusade 'in Tavastia' (Tampere/Hämeenlinna) to protect it from unidentified raiders – possibly Russians, but probably other Finns.
1240	'Swedish' attack on Novgorod is thwarted in the Battle of the Neva by Prince Alexander 'Nevsky', named for his victory.
1248 –1250	Second Swedish Crusade brings most of Finland under Swedish political control.
1293	Third Swedish Crusade leads to the conquest of Karelia and the establishment of Viipuri Castle.

1300	Consecration of the cathedral of Turku, Finland's original capital.
1319	Reign of King Magnus IV Ericson of Sweden.
1323	Treaty of Pähkinäsaari defines Finland's eastern border as a line drawn between the future site of St Petersburg and Oulu.
1346	A deal between bishops places the borders of the dioceses of Uppsala and Turku at Tornio, later used to mark the boundary between Finland and Sweden.
1353	The Black Death reaches Finland, killing an estimated third of its population.
1356	Reign of King Eric XII of Sweden.
1362	Reign of King Hacon of Sweden.
1364	Reign of King Albert of Sweden.
1389	Reign of Queen Margaret of Denmark, Norway, and Sweden (including Finland).
1396	Reign of King Eric XIII.
1397	The Kalmar Union – Finland is the easternmost march of a united Fenno-Scandinavia, but is marginalised by the move of the overall capital to Denmark.
1441	Reign of King Christopher.
1448	Reign of King Charles VIII.
1457	Reign of King Christian I.
1497	Reign of King John II.
1520	Reign of King Christian II 'the Tyrant'.
1523	Reign of King Gustav I Vasa, end of Kalmar Union.

1524	Gustav Vasa splits from the Church of Rome; beginnings of Lutheranism as the state religion of Sweden and Finland.
1548	Mikael Agricola translates the New Testament into Finnish. Beginning of Finnish as a written language.
1550	Founding of Helsingfors (Helsinki), as a colony of new settlers from Hälsingaland in Sweden.
1557	The English sea captain Stephen Borrough draws up a list of ninety-six Saami words. Beginnings of Saami as a written language.
1560	Reign of King Eric XIV.
1562	Katarina Jagellonica, the Polish wife of the Duke of Finland, introduces Turku to foreign innovations including the fork and the napkin.
1569	Reign of King Johan III of Sweden, former Duke of Finland. The deposed mad King Eric XIV is imprisoned in several castles, including Turku.
1590	Tsar Boris Godunov invades Finland, initiating the Russo-Swedish War.
1592	Reign of King Sigismund of Sweden.
1596	Peasant uprising known as the War of Clubs, suppressed in 1597 by Clas Fleming.
1604	Reign of King Karl IX of Sweden.
1611	Reign of King Gustav II Adolf of Sweden.
1617	Treaty of Stolbova leaves Karelia in Swedish hands.

1632	Reign of Queen Christina of Sweden.
1642	First publication of the entire Bible in Finnish.
1654	Reign of King Karl X Gustav of Sweden.
1655	The largely Finnish colony of 'New Sweden' in Delaware passes into Dutch hands.
1660	Reign of King Karl XI of Sweden.
1669	The Long Finn Rebellion in America is an early opposition to English rule.
1673	Joannis Schefferus writes his book *Lapponia*, at least partly to dispel rumours that the Swedish crown is employing Saami sorcerers in its foreign wars.
1673	Swedish proclamation states that Saami and farmers each have equal right to dwell in Lapland. Effective beginning of the colonisation of Saami lands in the north.
1695	Great Famine of Finland, also known as The Years of Many Deaths, in which 15–20% of the Finnish population perishes in just twenty-four months.
1697	Reign of King Karl XII of Sweden.
1700	Great Northern War between Sweden (and its allies) and Russia (and its allies).
1718	Reign of Queen Ulrika Eleonora of Sweden.
1720	Reign of King Frederick I of Sweden, with Ulrika as queen consort.

1721	Great Northern War ends with Sweden's loss of its territories on the south shore of the Gulf of Finland (including modern-day Estonia), and parts of Karelia (known as 'Old Finland' in Russia).
1751	Reign of King Adolf Frederick of Sweden.
1756	First legal restriction on home-brewed alcohol.
1771	Reign of King Gustav III of Sweden.
1792	Reign of King Gustav IV Adolf, last Swedish monarch to rule Finland.
1808	Outbreak of the Finnish War between Sweden and Russia. Russian forces occupy Finland.
1809	Finland becomes a Grand Duchy of Russia, under Tsar Alexander I.
1812	Helsinki becomes the new capital of Finland. The eastern lands of 'Old Finland' (lost in earlier wars) are restored to the Finnish Grand Duchy in order to streamline administration.
1819	The Scottish Quaker James Finlayson sees the Tampere rapids, and applies for permission to build a cotton mill powered by the waters.
1823	James Finlayson completes his first factory in Tampere.
1825	Nicholas I becomes Tsar.

1827	The Great Fire of Turku destroys Finland's largest town. Many institutions, including the university, are permanently relocated to Helsinki, hastening Turku's decline from its former prominence.
1835	First edition of Elias Lönnrot's *Kalevala*.
1836	James Finlayson sells his interest in the Tampere cotton mills, which retain his name.
1848	Publication of *The Tales of Ensign Stål* by Johan Ludvig Runeberg.
	First performance of the de facto Finnish national anthem 'Maamme' ('Our Land'), with lyrics by Runeberg and tune by Fredrik Pacius.
1849	Revised edition of the *Kalevala*.
1852	In Guovdageaidnu (Kautokeino), Norway, a group of Saami religious fanatics kill a merchant and policeman. Retroactively cited as the first event of Saami dissent.
1853	Outbreak of the Crimean War.
	Laestadians are ordered to have their own separate church services: effective beginning of Laestadianism as a distinct splinter from Christianity.
1854	In order to blockade St Petersburg and divert Russian forces from Crimea, an Anglo-French squadron attacks targets in the Baltic Sea, including controversial bungled raids on the Finnish coast.

1855	Anglo-French siege and bombardment of the naval fortress at Suomenlinna. Alexander II becomes 'the Good Tsar'. End of Crimean War.
1856	The Saimaa Canal connects Finland's largest lake and its tributaries to the sea at Viipuri.
1860	Russian rouble replaced by the Finnish markka as local currency.
1865	A wood-pulp mill is founded by Frederik Idestam in Tampere.
1866	A wet summer and hard winter lead to a new famine, recorded in Finnish accounts as the Great Hunger Years. 15–20% of the Finnish population dies by 1868.
1868	To secure hydroelectric power, Idestam relocates his mill to the nearby town of Nokia. The company takes its name from its new location.
1870	Lapland Gold Rush. Railway opens between Helsinki and St Petersburg.
1872	Helsinki University admits female students if they have a special dispensation.
1875	Publication of *The Book of Our Country*, by Topelius.
1877	The Plevna weaving hall in Tampere is the largest in the Nordic countries, with 1,200 power looms. It is the first in Finland to be fitted with electric lighting.
1881	Assassination of Alexander II. Succeeded by Alexander III.

1894	Death of Alexander III. Nicholas II becomes Tsar.
1898	Eduard Polón founds the Finnish Rubber Works (Gummitehdas).
1899	The February Manifesto of Nicholas II asserts his right to rule Finland without consulting native authorities. Beginning of the unpopular Russification policies.
1900	The Language Manifesto mandates Russian as the language for Finnish institutions. Sibelius completes his *Finlandia* symphony.
1901	Conscription Law obliges Finns to serve in the Russian army. Female university students are no longer required to apply for a special dispensation.
1902	Nokia adds electrical generation to its portfolio.
1903	Governor-General of Finland granted dictatorial powers.
1904	Assassination of Governor-General Nikolai Bobrikov.
1905	*John Grafton* incident and defeat for Russia in the Russo-Japanese War. First Russian Revolution leads to promises of reform.
1912	Arid Wickström founds the Finnish Cable Company.
1916	Finnish Jaeger volunteers fight for Germany; they will eventually return home to fight on the White side in the civil war.

1917	Second Russian Revolution; outbreak of Finnish revolution/civil war. Finland declares independence from Russia.
1918	Otto Kuusinen declares the Finnish Socialist Workers' Republic, flees to Russia after his defeat by the Whites.
1919	Prohibition (Kieltolaki) restricts access of Finns to liquor.
1926	First Finnish radio broadcasts.
1932	Official end of alcohol Prohibition laws.
1934	First edition of *Sápmelaš*, the first Saami newspaper in Finland.
1937	The use of the Finnish language is banned in Soviet Karelia.
1939	Frans Eemil Sillanpää wins Nobel Prize for Literature.
	Outbreak of Winter War against Soviets (ends 1940).
	Otto Kuusinen proclaims the Finnish Democratic Republic in Terijoki.
1941	Outbreak of Continuation War against Soviets (ends 1944). Finns and Nazis recapture much of Karelia, only to lose it once more.
	Veikko Koskienniemi writes lyrics to accompany the hymn section of Sibelius's *Finlandia*.
1944	Lapland War against the Nazis. Destruction of most buildings north of Rovaniemi (ends 1945).

1945	*The Moomins and the Great Flood*, first of the Moomin books, originally published in Swedish.
1946	First Finnish radio broadcasts in Saami.
1948	Friendship, Cooperation and Mutual Assistance Treaty with Soviet Union.
1952	Helsinki Olympics unfortunately leads to the invention of the *lonkero*.
1953	Finland's first Chinese restaurant.
1956–81	Urho Kekkonen is president for much of the Cold War.
1958	First Finnish television broadcasts.
1960	Saami Affairs Committee founded to implement Finnish Saami policy at a ministerial level.
1967	Nokia, the Finnish Rubber Works, and the Finnish Cable Company merge to form the Nokia Corporation. Its newly founded electronics division will run at a loss for the next fifteen years.
1968	Finland's first pizza restaurant.
1971	Nokia initiates its Finnish network for 'car-phone radios'. Homosexuality is decriminalised.
1977	Saami television broadcasts in Finland now run out of dedicated facilities in Inari. A new anti-discrimination law forbids restaurants from refusing entry to unaccompanied ladies.
1978	Finland's first Japanese restaurant.

1981	Homosexuality is dropped from the health authority's list of mental illnesses.
1982–94	Mauno Koivisto is Finland's president through the collapse of the Warsaw Pact.
1984	Nokia buys its main telecommunications competitor, Salora. Nokia's Mobira Talkman 'portable' phone retails at roughly US$ 6,000.
1986	Design approved for a Saami flag.
1987	'Second generation' mobile technology, which allows international roaming and transmission of data (i.e. text messaging), brought in with Nokia's Global System for Mobile Technology (GSM) – internationally adopted.
1990	*Happy Moomin Family*, the third Japanese iteration of the Moomin cartoons, starts a 'Moomin Boom', leading to increased Finland tourism, particularly among the Japanese.
1991	Helsinki University student Linus Torvalds begins work on his own operating system, later known as Linux. Beginning of Finland's association with open-source software.
1992	Finns gain right to use the Saami language in dealings with the authorities in Lapland, although proficiency in the Saami language is only 'recommended' for those same authorities.

1993	Finland founds a Saami Parliament for limited home rule.
1994–2000	Martti Ahtisaari is president of Finland.
1995	Finland joins the European Union. Law on Cultural Self-Government puts funding and control for local education in the hands of Saami. Social and health services added in 2002.
1998	Nokia is the world's largest mobile phone manufacturer, and remains so for the next fourteen years. Santa Park opens near Rovaniemi.
1999	First Finnish euros minted.
2000–12	Tarja Halonen is president of Finland.
2000	Helsinki is the European Capital of Culture.
2001	Legalisation of same-sex civil partnerships.
2002	Official date of the replacement of the Finnish markka with the euro.
2004	An amendment to the Finnish Nuclear Energy Act requires all nuclear waste created in Finland to be disposed of in Finland.
2005	Silvio Berlusconi proclaims that Finnish food is awful.
2006	Lordi wins the Eurovision Song Contest with 'Hard Rock Hallelujah'.
2007	Android and Apple iPhones bring lethal competition to Nokia in the mobile telecoms market.

2008	The Finnish-made 'Berlusconi' pizza forces Italy into second place in an international competition. Martti Ahtisaari receives the Nobel Peace Prize.
2009	Release of the first game in the *Angry Birds* franchise. Karelian is recognised as a separate minority language, spoken by 5,000 Finns. The University Act pushes institutes of higher education towards 'applied' research.
2011	Turku is the European Capital of Culture.
2012–14	Supercell's *Clash of Clans* is the most popular video game in the world.
2013–25	Sauli Niinistö is president of Finland
2014	Nokia's mobile phone business, the only major part left after the company divested itself of most other businesses in the 1990s, is sold to Microsoft.
2015	Final broadcast of *Finland Calling*, the Finnish-language TV programme in Michigan's Upper Peninsula. Legalisation of same-sex marriage.
2016	After widespread layoffs, Microsoft sells off its underperforming Microsoft Mobile (formerly Nokia).
2017	Centenary of the foundation of the Finnish republic.
2019	The Neo-Nazi 'Nordic Resistance Movement' is banned in Finland.
2020	Finland weathers the COVID-19 pandemic.

2022	The long-delayed third reactor at Olkiluoto comes online. Finland applies to join NATO; Russia cuts gas supplies.
2025	Lahti scheduled to meet its target to become Finland's first carbon-neutral town.
2026	Oulu is the European Capital of Culture.

Further Reading and References

Unless my main text is quoting from an untranslated source, all the books listed here are available in English. Many books concerning Finland are inadequately tagged by online booksellers, and only show up on searches if one directly requests them. Truly dedicated or interested readers are advised to browse the 'Fennica' sections in Finnish bookshops, which often have English-language translations of local books. Local museums and university bookstores are also liable to have locally produced, small-press translations of books and theses that have never reached the attention of Amazon. My sources in this paperback edition rely to a larger extent on works in the Finnish language, mentioned here if they formed a significant contribution to my main text.

Guidebooks

There's nothing to fault the chunky *Lonely Planet: Finland* guide, most recently updated in 2018 and handily now available on Kindle. The tourist who truly wants to investigate the forgotten corners of the country might like to invest in the harder-to-find *Finland: A Cultural Guide* (Otava, 2003) by Pirkko-Liisa Louhenjoki-Schulman and Kaius Hedenström, which not only roots out the obscure art collections and craft centres, but also offers numerous illustrations to pique the interest and help the confused traveller. Jorma Tuomi-Nikula and Altti Holmroos are the authors of *Finnish Inland Waters and Archipelago in the Wake of the Czars* (Kristina Cruises, 2003), which offers an English-language précis of Tuomi Nikula's earlier Finnish-language book on the vacationing Tsars. It is an informative bilingual booklet about the routes taken by company cruise ships from Helsinki, way out west to the Åland Islands, and then all the way east on the Gulf of Finland to Viipuri, and up through the Saimaa canal as far as Savonlinna.

Publishers and Authors

Finns are avid readers, in several languages, although the small size of the population can make local books expensive. Many Finnish towns boast branches of Suomalainen Kirjakauppa ('The Finnish Bookshop') and a handful of surviving branches of Akateeminen Kirjakauppa ('The Academic Bookshop'), both of which are sure to have an impressive selection of English-language novels and magazines. Many Finnish authors have been translated into English, as worthy literati, earnest representatives, or participants in the modern fad for Nordic Noir. There are, in fact, so many available once you start looking that a small book such as this can only barely scratch the surface. Hard to find in English, but immensely influential on the Finns, is Johan Ludvig Runeberg's *Tales of Ensign Stål* (English trans. WSOY, 1952). Originally published in Swedish between 1848 and 1860, and recounting the events of the war that cost Sweden its Eastland, it has been translated four times into *Finnish* to reflect changes in language and attitude. It was a set text in schools in both Finland and Sweden.

During the Winter War, it was reprinted and given away free to soldiers to instil a sense of nationalist spirit. Some of its opening verses, 'Maamme' ('Our Land'), were set to music and form the basis of Finland's national anthem.

Oh our land, Finland, land of our birth,
Rings out the golden word!
No valley, no hill,
No water, shore more dear
Than this northern homeland,
Precious land of our fathers.
Your splendour from its shell
One day will bloom;
From our love shall rise
Your hope, glorious joy,
And once your song, fatherland
Higher still will echo.

Runeberg is celebrated in many monuments throughout Finland, and in the Runeberg Tart, one of the stodgy confections of which the Finns are inexplicably proud. He is oddly unrepresented in the English language despite his importance; he not only gave Finland a martial epic of the end of the Swedish era, but also *The Elk Hunters* – the first valorisation of the common man in Finland, kicking off a rich vein of national literature, and *King Fjalar*, an 'Ossianic' poem, which is to say, a fake history that might well have defined a whole generation of Finnish art if the *Kalevala* hadn't come along and trumped it.

'In the beginning, there was the marsh, the hoe, and

Jussi'. With such a simple, cinematic sentence, zooming in on the lone crofter draining a swamp to break new farmland, Vainö Linna commences his three-volume epic *Under the North Star* (Aspasia, 2001–3). Encompassing several generations, from the closing days of Russian rule to the aftermath of the Second World War, it charts the fortunes of the Koskela family as they create their homestead out of wilderness and then stand their ground against predatory authorities, civil strife, and economic hardship.

Linna was one of the most influential Finnish authors of the twentieth century, in part for his controversial book *The Unknown Soldier* (WSOY, 1968). The abridged English edition lacks much of the feather-ruffling effect of the 1954 original, in which Linna drew on his own experiences in the Continuation War. Linna's soldiers are preoccupied with staying alive and hanging on to their dugout – an action-oriented, subjective touch that was deeply out-of-step with other mythologies of the war, which would have their readers believe that everybody was a hero fighting out of deep-seated political convictions and a grasp of the bigger picture. In 2000, an earlier draft was published under his original title of *Sotaromaani* ('A War Novel'). Even more critical of the establishment and cynical about 'why we fight', it is sadly unavailable in English.

Tove Jansson remains a popular point of entry for foreign readers, although the author confesses that her world-famous Moomin stories leave her cold. The more one knows about Jansson's life, the more they look like extended Mary-Sue diaries, in which Jansson alleviates boredom in a summer shack by pretending all her lovers, family members, and house-guests are eccentric trolls. Boel Westin's *Tove Jansson: Life, Art, Words – the Authorised Biography* (Sort Of Books, 2013) offers a more thorough portrayal of this most famous of Swedish-speaking Finns, whose books for adults are often overlooked. For a glimpse of her skills outside the children's market, see *Travelling Light*, *The Listener*, or her autobiography *Sculptor's Daughter: A Childhood Memoir*.

Written originally in Czech, Markéta Hejkalová's *Mika Waltari: the Finn* (WSOY, 2007) examines the career of the unassuming novelist who was once an international superstar. It is a firm reminder of how Anglophone success is not everything – Waltari has been translated into over forty languages, although his historical epics such as *The Roman* and *The Etruscan* are little-known in English. *The Egyptian* was made into a film starring Yul Brynner, but Waltari sometimes seems excluded from the conversation on Finnish literature, because unlike many of his contemporaries, he rarely wrote on the Matter of Finland. He found pharaohs more interesting than farmers, and in the long run, that may have cost him his place in the Finnish hall of fame. Some of his most 'Finnish' works, in fact, were written for the screen, including *The February Manifesto* (1939), which was incendiary enough to be banned for several decades in the Cold War era in order to avoid antagonising the Russians.

Several Finnish crime novelists have managed to clamber aboard the translation bandwagon for Nordic Noir, including Jarko Sipilä with his Helsinki Homicide series, and Harri Nykänen's *Raid* books – the latter featuring one of the most Finnish men imaginable, a good-hearted hitman who duels with evil Swedes in battles of wits, before sloping off to the forest to barbecue a celebratory sausage.

Antti Tuominen's *The Healer* (Vintage, 2013) straddles the line between thriller and science fiction, set in a near future Helsinki depopulated by climate change. As one might expect from the country whose very sense of self was bootstrapped out of a fantasy book, Finland's speculative fiction community is a busy bunch, most ably represented on the international stage by Johanna Sinisalo, author of *Troll* and *The Blood of Angels*. She is also the editor of the *Book of Finnish Fantasy* (Dedalus, 2005), which along with Desirina Boskovich's *It Came From the North* (Cheeky Frawg, 2013) offers a rogue's gallery of the genre's Finnish movers and shakers.

Finland also forms a backdrop for many novels by foreigners, such as Elizabeth Hand's *Available Dark* (Minotaur, 2012), in which a photographer goes on the trail of heavy metal murders. It is a location for both the film and original book of Len Deighton's *Billion-Dollar Brain* (Cape, 1966), and makes little impression in Raymond Benson's abysmal *Icebreaker* (Cape, 1983) in which James Bond visits Helsinki and singularly fails to evoke any sense of place or character.

General Accounts

The chunkiest and most in-depth general account in English is Eino Jutikkala and Kauko Pirinen's *A History of Finland* (WSOY, 2003), now in its sixth edition. Henrik Meinander's acclaimed *A History of Finland* (OUP, 2021) has been recently updated. More concise, but wonderfully detailed and significantly cheaper, is Fred Singleton's *A Short History of Finland* (Cambridge University Press, 1998), released by a publisher bafflingly competing with itself in the form of David Kirby's *A Concise History of Finland* (Cambridge University Press, 2006). Originally written by George Maude, but updated in its new edition by Titus Hjelm, *The Historical Dictionary of Finland* (Scarecrow, 2021) is an expensive but exhaustive selection of Finnish facts.

It is worth mentioning here, as well, that most back issues of the *Journal of Finnish Studies*, including entire special issues on many of the subjects covered in this book, are available online as PDFs under a welcome Open Access policy. See: https://www.shsu.edu/eng_ira/finnishstudies/JoFS_Covers.html

Places and Encounters

The seasoned Finland visitor will find much to enjoy in Tony Lurcock's surveys of a particular kind of foreign tourist. His *Not So Barren or Uncultivated: British Travellers in Finland 1760–1830* (CB Editions, 2010), and its sequels *No Particular Hurry: British Travellers in Finland 1830–1917* (CB Editions, 2013), *A Life of Extremes: The British Discover Modern Finland 1917–1941* (CB Editions, 2015) and *Finish Off with Finland: A Miscellany* (CB Editions, 2021), collate a lifetime's collecting of obscure letters and journals, and mining them for their most pertinent or humorous soundbites – any travellers' quotes in this book not named in this bibliography are liable to have been lifted from Lurcock's anthologies.

For a more modern tour of the country, Robert Goldstein's *Riding With Reindeer: A Bicycle Ride Through Finland, Lapland and Arctic Norway* (Rivendell, 2011) sweetly recounts his numerous encounters with various winding roads, unexpectedly hilly dales, and politely disbelieving Finns as he cycles across the whole country in a haphazard zigzag.

Arts and Crafts

The most crucial work of Finnish culture in the nineteenth century is surely Elias Lönnrot's *Kalevala* (OUP, 1999), which only truly comes alive once one has seen the forests and lakes, and heard the rhythm of spoken Finnish at first hand. His later *Magic Songs of the Finns* (repr. Pagan Archive, 2011) is a detailed and cross-referenced collection of spells and stories, origin myths and curses, offering the curious reader everything from charms to protect against bears to bogglingly graphic spells to ease the pain of childbirth. He also lists kennings – poetic allusions – that recur in Finnish poetry, that speak volumes themselves with such revelations that a wolf was an 'Estonian cur', and a cockroach, somewhat less evocatively, was a 'six-footed, ball-shaped thing'.

Susanna Petterson's edited collection *Stories of Finnish Art* (Ateneum/Hatje Cantz, 2016) is the best place to start when looking for details about Finland's artists. Among many artistic biographies and collections, *Akseli Gallen-Kallela: Artist and Visionary* (WSOY, 1994, English text by Michael Wynne-Ellis) goes to the heart of Finnish National Romanticism. For a quirkier view, that investigates the use of one particular national icon in art, cartoons, and political satire, see Johanna Valenius's *Undressing the Maid: Gender, Sexuality and the Body in the Construction of the Finnish Nation* (SKS, 2004). My comments on Tolkien's *Story of Kullervo* derive from the annotated edition, edited by Verlyn Flieger (Harper Collins, 2015).

Prehistory to 1159

There is remarkably little in English on Finnish prehistory; my main source is Matti Huurre's *9000 Vuotta Suomen esihistoriaa* (Otava, 2004). A general Arctic account, which includes Finland, can be found in John Hoffecker's *A Prehistory of the North: Human Settlement of the Higher Latitudes* (Rutgers, 2004). Otherwise, the best starting point is likely to be some of the anthropological materials listed below in the Saami section.

For a precise and granular assessment of the degree to which the Vikings were part of Finnish history, I recommend Joonas Ahola et al's *Fibula, Fabula, Fact: The Viking Age in Finland* (SKS, 2014). As noted in my main text, Lee Hollander's *Heimskringla: History of the Kings of Norway* (University of Texas, 1964) is the most accurate version, which refuses to sacrifice meaning and tone in favour of rhymes. In the Finnish language, Mikko Moilanen's *Viikinkimiekat Suomessa* (SKS, 2018) offers an exhaustive overview of the context and conditions of swords from before, during and after the Viking age, recovered by Finnish archaeologists.

Swedish Finland: 1159–1809

The best account of the Christianisation of the Nordic countries is Eric Christiansen's *The Northern Crusades* (Penguin, 1997), although it covers all the Baltic, not merely the region now known as Finland. But since the Finns for much of this period were intimately involved with the history of Sweden itself, as subjects of the Swedish crown, the best place to understand the Gustavs and the Adolfs of the era is somewhere like *A Concise History of Sweden* (Cambridge University Press, 2008), by Neil Kent. Karl XII, 'last of the Vikings', and his amazing life in the saddle are covered in great depth in Robert Nisbet Bain's *Charles XII and the Collapse of the Swedish Empire* (Putnam, 1895), now widely available in facsimile and e-Book reprints. For a more modern take on the era when Finnish cavalrymen fought at the edges of the Ottoman Empire, Gary Dean Peterson's *Warrior Kings of Sweden* (McFarland, 2007) has plenty of swashbuckling and scandal.

Aboa vetus et nova (SKS, 2005) is a large format book in four parallel languages – the original Latin of Daniel Juslenius, as well as Finnish, Swedish, and English. A Master's thesis from 1700, seeking to reclaim as much lost history as possible after the destruction of the Duchy archives in a fire at Kuusisto in 1439, it remains one of the richest sources on medieval Finland, particularly Turku. For a glimpse of some of the activities in the period's wars, Reijo Heikkinen's *Kajaani Castle* (Kainuu Museum, 2005) approaches through the rise and fall of the titular site. Matti Laamanen and Hanna-Leena Prusi achieve something similar with *Olavinlinna Castle* (National Board of Antiquities, 2007), which details everything to be found at Savonlinna's titular keep.

Reimund Kvideland and Henning Sehmsdorf's *Scandanavian Folk Belief and Legend* (Minnesota University Press, 1988) includes many folktales from Swedish-speaking Finland, relics of the period when the country was a Swedish province. As for the frictions caused by the annexation of 'Old Finland', along with its population of Orthodox believers, see Raisa Maria Toivo's *Faith and Magic in Early Modern Finland* (Palgrave, 2016).

For the crazy story of the involvement of Finns in early American revolution, I have leaned on Evan Haefeli's article in *The Pennsylvania Magazine of History and Biography* (April 2006), 'The Revolt of the Long Swede [*sic*]: Transatlantic Hopes and Fears on the Delaware, 1669'.

Russian Finland: 1809–1917

Nineteenth century Finland's greatest foreign chronicler is Mrs Alec Tweedie, the casually racist but often insightful woman of letters, whose *Through Finland in Carts* (Thomas Nelson & Sons, 1897) remains oddly up-to-date in its assessment of the Finnish character. The bulk of her observations are about Finnish people and the natural world, and richly rewarding to the modern visitor because so little appears to have changed.

The story of the Crimean War in the Baltic is told in exhaustive detail by Basil Greenhill and Ann Giffard in *The British Assault on Finland 1854–1855: A Forgotten Naval War* (Conway, 1988).

The story of Russian Finland is also the story of the

development of Finnish nationalism, particularly through the compilation, publication, and reception of Elias Lönnrot's *Kalevala*. Juha Pentikäinen's *Kalevala Mythology* (Indiana University Press, 1999) is not only an in-depth guide to the epic itself, but also an incisive biography of its author and the very personal experiences and inspirations that inspired his text. *Sibelius: A Composer's Life and the Awakening of Finland* (University of Chicago Press, 2009) does much the same thing for the music of Finland's national composer.

For anyone looking for a truly deep study of the period, Derek Fewster's *Visions of Past Glory: Nationalism and the Construction of Early Finnish History* (Finnish Literature Society, 2005) picks apart the different strands and applications of Finnish national identity, not only during the Russian period but also in the twentieth century as the Finns struggled to reconcile their changing political situation to similarly variable historical records and artistic works. Fewster identifies shades of meaning and interpretation that a book like this one can only hint at. Tuomo Polvinen's *Imperial Borderland: Bobrikov and the Attempted Russification of Finland* (Hurst, 1995) is similarly comprehensive on the complex politics of the late nineteenth century, as Russia's tightening fist caused so much goodwill to slip from its grasp. Eino Parmanen's *Taistelujen Kirja* (WSOY, 1936) or *Book of the Struggles* is sadly not available in English but is an exhaustive four-volume account of Finland's long road towards a republic.

As for the adventures of Finns in the Far East, they are often buried in the footnotes of histories of Siberia and

Russian Alaska, such as Mark Bassin's *Imperial Visions: Nationalist Imagination and Geographical Expansion in the Russian Far East, 1840–1865* (Cambridge University Press, 1999). Fridolf Höök is the leading subject of Toivo Koivisto's *Suomalaista Sisua Villissä Idässä* (Gummerus, 1947).

There is an entire sub-genre of publishing devoted to the experience of Finns in America, but I recommend Auvo Kostiainen's edited collection *Finns in the United States: A History of Settlement, Dissent and Integration* (Michigan State University Press, 2015) not only for its varied approaches and illuminating anecdotes, but for the treasure trove in its bibliography. There are further stories to be found in Armas Holmio's *History of the Finns in Michigan* (Wayne State University Press, 2001). The song 'To America, to America' can be found in Leea Virtanen and Thomas DuBois' *Finnish Folklore* (SKS, 2000).

Finland in the early Twentieth Century

Anthony Upton's *The Finnish Revolution 1917–1918* (University of Minnesota Press, 1980) is a chunky 600-page account of the upheaval also known as the Finnish Civil War, rich with anecdotes and detail. In more recent times Tuomas Tepora and Aapo Roselius's edited collection *The Finnish Civil War 1918: History, Memory, Legacy* (Brill, 2014) offers rich insights into the upheavals and historical footprint of the birth of the Finnish republic. Very little about the Reds exists, since those most likely to commemorate them were either dead in 1918, exiles in Russia, or emigrants to the USA and elsewhere. There is, however, Petri Haapala et al.'s *Tampere 1918: A Town in the Civil*

War (Vapriikki, 2010), published by the town museum, crammed with evocative photographs and essays on the various elements of the war and its aftermath, as well as Risto Alapuro's far-left *State and Revolution in Finland* (Haymarket Books, 2018), which characterises 1918 as a 'failed' revolution that didn't go far enough.

Rüdiger von der Goltz, a leader of the German troops in Finland during the civil war, published his memoirs of the period as *My Mission in Finland and the Baltic* (Koehler, 1920); translator Peter Kalnin published the entire work as an e-book in 2013, available from Amazon.

The sorry tale of the rush to cook up a Finnish king is best told in English in Michael Nash's article 'The Last King of Finland' (Royalty Digest 2012: 1). A far more in-depth account, only available in Finnish, is Martti Santavuori's *Suomen kuningas* (Karisto, 1965).

My own *Mannerheim: President, Soldier, Spy* (Haus, 2009) is a biography of Finland's most famous leader, including his early life in Russian military service, his leadership of the White forces in the civil war, and his triumphant days as the Marshal of Finland.

For the further adventures of Finnish-Americans in the twentieth century, Samira Saramo's *Building That Bright Future: Soviet Karelia in the Life Writing of Finnish North Americans* (University of Toronto, 2022) and Alexey Golubev and Irina Takala's *The Search for a Socialist El Dorado: Finnish Immigration to Soviet Karelia from the United States and Canada in the 1930s* (Michigan State University, 2014) are both lively accounts of the idealism, struggles and eventual betrayal of the thousands of ethnic

Finns who returned to Europe to take part in the creation of a new world in what had once been 'Old Finland'.

Finland at War

Finland's wartime history is told in many books, although perhaps the most comprehensive in English is William Trotter's *Winter War* (Aurum, 2003, released earlier in the US as *A Frozen Hell*). The best of recent scholarship on the subject is collated in Tiina Kinnunen and Ville Kivimäki's *Finland in World War II: History, Memory, Interpretations* (Brill, 2012). I also highly recommend Oula Seitsonen's *Archaeologies of Hitler's Arctic War: Heritage of the Second World War Military Presence in Arctic Lapland* (Routledge, 2020), and Muir and Worthen's *Finland's Holocaust: Silences of History* (Palgrave Macmillan, 2013), which delves into more nuanced and complex detail into Finland's engagement with, whatever the prime minister's wartime denials, something that might definitely be described as a 'Jewish question'. For a very different account of the conflict in Lapland, framed not as an us-vs-them account, but as a stern commentary from the local Saami, who saw it as a spat between two equally unwelcome sets of colonisers, see Veli-Pekka Lehtola's *Surviving the Upheaval of the Arctic War: Evacuation and Return of the Sámi People in Sápmi During and After the Second World War* (Puntsi, 2019).

Once into the rarefied realms of military publishing, there is an embarrassment of riches about Finnish armaments and vehicles, and stirring tales of veterans and soldiers. British readers might like to seek out Justin Brooke's obscure book on his wartime experiences, *The Volunteers:*

The Full Story of the British Volunteers in Finland 1939–41 (Self Publishing Association, 1990). Tellingly, it had a mass-market publication in its original Finnish edition, but limped out from a vanity press in the author's homeland. More farce than force, it tells the tale of several hundred British men, many deemed unfit for service at home, others instilled with a romantic notion of fighting Communists, who formed a volunteer detachment and shipped out to Finland, only to discover that the Winter War was already over. The men see no action, at least of a military nature, although there are anecdotes galore about their adventures, including a drunken and unforgettably misguided attempt to curry favour with a waitress in Jyväskylä by buying her a pair of French knickers.

For the Cold War 'deep state', I have had to rely on Finnish-language sources, including Ohto Manninen and Lauri Lehtonen's *Stella Polariksen perintö* (Docendo, 2019). Matti Lukkari's *Asekätkentä* (Otava, 1984) tells the whole jaw-dropping, how-is-this-not-a-movie tale of the Weapons Cache Conspiracy. For the fate of those Finns who believed the Soviet dream, look no further than Mayme Sevander and Laurie Hertzel's *They Took My Father: Finnish Americans in Stalin's Russia* (Minnesota University Press, 2004) and Nick Baron's *Soviet Karelia: Politics, Planning and Terror in Stalin's Russia, 1920–1939* (Routledge, 2012).

The Saami and Lapland
Various orthographies write their name as the Saami or the Sámi, so get used to calling them that, rather than 'Lapps', which they regard as racist and derogatory – Lapland

implies a location on the periphery, so a Lapp is by definition an outsider.

In terms of chunky books on Everything You Need to Know About the Saami, *The Saami: A Cultural Encyclopaedia* (SKS, 2005), edited by Ulla-Maija Kulonen, Irja Seurujärvi-Kari and Risto Pulkkinen is hard to beat. Its 500 pages offer entries on everything from *afruvvá* ('mermaids') to *yoik* ('song') and all parts in between. For a more narrative account, Veli-Pekka Lehtola's *The Sámi People: Traditions in Transition* (Puntsi, 2004) offers a concise history of the people of Lapland, from their earliest mentions in classical geographies, to their modern struggles over identity and representation.

Finland Today

Although it begins with the newly independent state in 1918, the bulk of George Maude's *Aspects of the Governing of the Finns* (Peter Lang, 2010) is concerned with the often-overlooked period of the Cold War – it is particularly good on the brinkmanship of the Kekkonen era, which is a fundamental cornerstone of Finnish historical memory, but unknown to outsiders. Carl-Gustav Lindén's *Kingdom of Nokia: How a Nation Served the Needs of One Company* (Helsinki University Press, 2021), is a book-length account of Finland's most famous corporation.

For coverage of history as revealed in Finnish food and drink, I have leaned on Finnish sources, particularly Ritva Kylli's *Suomen Ruokahistoria: Suolihasta sushiin* (Gaudeamus, 2021) and Jonna Pulkinen's *Kieltolaki: Kielletyn viinan historia Suomessa* (Minerva, 2015). For the fate of the *Monument to Selfishness*, quotes are from the article by Katri Järvinen, '"Itsekkyyden muistomerkki" vanhentui Helsingin Linnunlaulussa harvinaisen nopeasti' (*Helsingin Sanomat*, 18 July 2020).

English subtitles are not forthcoming for local films in Finnish cinemas, but almost all modern Finnish films have English subtitles on their DVD release, and can present an interesting and enduring window into the culture. Pietari Kääpä's *Directory of World Cinema: Finland* (Intellect, 2012), offers an exhaustive run-down of the history, industry, and outlook of Finnish film, although some of his contributors seem oddly keen on wittering in academic cant, while neglecting to mention that the particular film they are discussing is tediously unwatchable. Real gluttons for punishment can check out my ongoing project to watch every Finnish film ever made in more or less chronological order, which began in the 2010s, over at www.schoolgirlm-ilkycrisis.com/tag/finnfilms. Currently wading through the 1940s, I expect to reach the end of the line in about ten years' time, although since the blog is set to publish a review only once a month, the public will not see the finish line until the 2040s.